WORCESTERSHIRE
FOLK
TALES

WORCESTERSHIRE
FOLK
TALES

DAVID PHELPS

The
History
Press

First published 2013

The History Press
The Mill, Brimscombe Port
Stroud, Gloucestershire, GL5 2QG
www.thehistorypress.co.uk

British Library Cataloguing in Publication Data.
A catalogue record for this book is available from the British Library.

ISBN 978 0 7524 8580 5

Typesetting and origination by The History Press
Printed in Great Britain

The ground holds the memory of all that has happened to it.

Hugh Lupton

CONTENTS

ACKNOWLEDGEMENTS

My grateful thanks to the staff of Hereford and Worcester libraries, who provided me with much useful research material. Long may they flourish. These are stories of the oral tradition, and were greatly improved by being told to the Much Dewchurch and Newent story circles. I am indebted to my fellow storytellers for their patience and advice. It is always good to keep things in the family, so I am immensely thankful to my daughter, Marina, for doing the illustrations for this book during a particularly busy period of her life. Thanks also to Jenny Briancourt and her colleagues at The History Press for commissioning this work and for their help through the process, and also to Katherine Soutar-Caddick for continuing to provide such stunning drawings for the series' covers.

INTRODUCTION

My grandfather was born in Suckley, Worcestershire, the son of cherry farmers. It sounds like an idyllic occupation, at least until you have care of such trees yourself; it quite puts you off blackbirds. Although he spent his married life in Herefordshire, he took his stories to my grandmother, and it was from her that I first discovered the power of stories.

Worcestershire is a complex county, partly facing the wild border lands and partly facing the industrialised West Midlands. Its stories reflect that complexity. The stories range from our mythical past to an unsolved twentieth-century murder, with plenty of double dealing and farce in between. Some might be familiar, but I hope some will be new and increase your feeling for the precious Worcestershire countryside. One story that is not here is the Legend of St Kenelm. That can be found in Anthony Nanson's excellent *Gloucestershire Folk Tales*. This is only fair because the monks of Winchcombe, Gloucestershire stole the body of the saint by subterfuge in the Middle Ages.

Once, we held the land sacred. This was sensible because it provided us with the means for our survival, both physically and spiritually. We admire the Australian aborigines for their knowledge of traditional songlines but, just a few centuries ago, our ancestors could also have told you how the landscape you moved in was alive with the memory of previous generations, the story of that house, what once happened in that field and why you had to take special care if you went into that wood at night. Where did we lose that sense of the sacred? Perhaps it was with the Enclosure Movement, where most of our ancestors lost a sense of owner- ship with the land. Perhaps it was with the Industrial Revolution, when many people moved away from day-to-day contact with the land and lost their sense of belonging. But I do not believe that feeling for the sacred has been lost forever. By telling the sto- ries of the land we can make it magical again.

An example of why we need these stories came when I was writing this book. Wychavon District Council proposed build- ing 200 houses on the meadow where Eof had his vision of Our Lady (*see* the story of St Egwin for the details of this event). Fortunately the people of Evesham know their local stories, and there have been many well-attended protest meetings against these plans. When you destroy a sacred site, you destroy something of your heart, so I can only hope that their stand is successful. It is still undecided at the time of writing.

ONE

THE HEDGEHOG
AND THE DEVIL

Once there was a very sporty hedgehog. Hedgehogs can be surprisingly quick on the ground when they want to be, and this young fellow prided himself on how fast he could go and the looks of astonishment that he left behind.

Such behaviour smacked of the sin of pride, and the other hedgehogs warned him that he should tone himself down a bit and take to scurrying about in the undergrowth, the way proper hedgehogs are supposed to behave, instead of always drawing attention to himself. It would lead to trouble they told him. Of course the young one, proud of showing off his hedgehog powers, did no such thing.

As luck would have it, one evening the Devil was walking in the Malverns. With such beautiful views over into Worcestershire, it always put him in a bad mood. He heard the laughter of the hedgehog as it outdistanced a very surprised badger. More specifically, he heard the pride in that laughter, and thought he would be able to make some mischief out of it. He did not have any hedgehogs in hell – they were not that sort of species – so he thought it would be very clever of him to get at least one. The Devil is not above a bit of pride himself.

So he sidled up to the hedgehog as it stood panting on the grass.

'You're a very fine runner,' complimented Old Nick.

'Thank you,' said the hedgehog, 'I think I am.'

'You do, don't you. But I can run faster.'

The hedgehog looked at the creature dressed all in black and with two wobbly legs ending in goat's feet. 'I'm sure that's not true.' he said.

'Well, there's only one way of testing it.' said the old 'un. 'We shall have to have a race. And the winner gets to choose anything in the loser's possession to have as his own for all eternity. Does that sound fair?'

The hedgehog, who was a little naive about the ways of the world, agreed that it was.

'Then let's meet here tomorrow at the same time, and we'll find out who is the fastest.' With that he went off with a bit more skip in his step than he had started out the day.

After he had gone, another hedgehog, the first's best friend, came out of the brambles where he had been hiding. 'What have you done? Do you know who that was?'

The sporty hedgehog shrugged his spines.

'That was him! You know, the Devil. He takes souls, and he roasts them down in Hell, and I'm sure that's what he means to do with you if he wins that race.'

Now the first hedgehog started to look a bit nervous. His spines drooped and he curled himself into a ball for comfort's sake.

'What am I going to do?' he wailed.

The second hedgehog thought for a moment. 'You've given me a bit of an idea. Come over here and I'll tell you about it.'

So the two hedgehogs stood face to face for some time talking and gradually huge smiles spread over both their faces.

The next day, the Devil was first to arrive at the spot. He waited impatiently for the hedgehog to turn up. When he finally did, the Devil stamped his hoof impatiently. 'I suspected you'd thought better of it,' he said. He was not going to be nearly as civil as he had been the previous day; he just wanted his prize.

'No, I've come.' said the hedgehog. 'Although I have been thinking; since you challenged me to the race, I ought to pick conditions.'

'I don't see any harm in that.'

'I'm a creature of the night, so let's run our race in the dark. Also I'm a timid creature, not used to open spaces. Let's run up and down that ditch over there until one of us has had enough.'

The Devil smiled. It was really pitiful if the hedgehog thought he was going to get any advantage that way. He had perfect night vision, and he was so confident that he could out-pace this proud animal that he agreed to those rules.

They waited for the evening to get darker, the Devil distracting himself with wondering what roast hedgehog tasted like. At last the hedgehog decided that it was sufficiently black for the race to begin, so they lined up in the ditch, checking that neither was ahead of the other. The Devil was surprised to see the hedgehog roll himself into a ball. He laughed. 'Does the stupid creature think he can roll faster than I can run?' he thought. 'This is going to be easy.'

'Right,' came the muffled voice of the hedgehog, 'When I say go, we start. Ready … steady … Go!'

The Devil set off, not going too fast, but confident that he had left the hedgehog well behind. So he was surprised when he got to the end of the ditch and found the hedgehog there ahead of him, still rolled in a ball. The hedgehog poked his snout out and cried, 'Off we go again!'

The Devil, chastened, turned round and set off, this time at a slightly faster pace. But, when he got to the beginning of the ditch, there was the damned hedgehog. 'Off we go again!' it cried, and the Devil had no choice but to turn around and run again.

So it went on throughout the night. The Devil ran faster and faster but still the hedgehog would be there before him shouting, 'Off we go again!'

By the time the first hints of dawn were lightening the east, and the cocks of Worcestershire were clearing their throats ready to start crowing, the Devil was getting heart-achingly sick of the whole proceedings. The next time he came up to the hedgehog and it lifted its head to say, 'Off we go again!' he reached out to strangle the creature, but instead got a handful of prickles. He let out a terrible yowl that quietened all the cocks just as they were about to let forth, said something that the young hedgehog did not understand and disappeared in a flash of blue smoke, leaving behind a strong smell of sulphur.

The two hedgehogs walked to meet each other in the middle of the ditch because, of course, that had been the hedgehog's idea: to station himself at the other end of the ditch, so that the Devil thought that he had been bested by the original hedgehog and so on through the night.

'The only thing is,' said the sporty hedgehog, 'now I suppose I will never get my prize, even though I won the contest.' His friend gave a deep sigh.

For many years after that, when people of the district were performing some repetitive task, they would say, 'Off we go again, as the hedgehog said to the Devil.'

Sadly, hedgehogs are not nearly as numerous as they once were in the countryside. Cars, modern farming practices and fences have drastically reduced their numbers. We should do what we can to help them, including not driving so fast at night, leaving some wild places in our gardens where hedgehogs can rest and making sure there are hedgehog-sized gaps in our boundary walls, so that they can get about their territory. We would also do well to leave out some cat food for them (in cat-proof containers) because they thrive on it. Strangely, the country custom of putting out bread and milk is not so good. It gives them the squits.

TWO

SABRINA

Geoffrey of Monmouth tells us that, after the sacking of Troy, a few survivors (under their leader, Brutus) went searching for a place where they could found a new Troy. After many adventures they arrived in Britain, which they considered the perfect place. The only thing wrong with it was that it was infested with a large number of giants. Fortunately the hero Corineus was able to get rid of them, but if you want to know how he did that, you will have to read Michael Dacre's *Devon Folk Tales* in this series, because much of it happened in Totnes.

To cut a long story short, Brutus divided his kingdom between his three sons. Locrinus was given England, Camber got Wales and Albanactus Scotland. Corineus, in recognition of his stalwart services, received Cornwall as his fiefdom. After Brutus' death, everyone agreed that it would be a wonderful thing if Locrinus were to marry Corineus's daughter Gwendolen.

So the island of Britain would have been at peace, and everyone could have got on with their lives, had Humber the Hun not chosen that moment to invade the north of the country. He defeated and killed Albanactus, and Locrinus was forced to suspend the marriage festivities and march north to meet the invaders.

A fierce battle took place in what is now north Lincolnshire. Eventually the Huns were defeated and Humber fled, only to drown in the river that still bears his name. Among the many captives taken was Humber's daughter, Estrildis. As soon as she was brought before him Locrinus found that he was a captive himself, disarmed by her beauty. Tall and blonde, in contrast to the short dumpy brunettes that Locrinus was used to, she stared at him coldly and unafraid, as if daring him to do anything to her. He knew immediately that this was the woman he was meant to marry.

When the news reached Corineus, he was naturally beside himself with anger. He, who had risked his life to rid the land of giants, had now been made a laughing stock by this stupid boy. He marched his army to London to confront the king. None of the royal bodyguard would stand up to him; after all, you tend not to want to get on the wrong side of a man who made his reputation by killing giants. Corineus strode into the king's feasting hall, smashed over a few tables and then grabbed Locrinus, holding him a couple of feet off the ground with his sharp battle axe against the King of England's throat. Then he started to negotiate on the wisdom of putting his daughter aside.

In the end it was decided that Locrinus would marry Gwendolen after all, and Estrildis would be sold into slavery. Locrinus was wise enough to know that he would have to keep part of the bargain – marrying Gwendolen – but he had no intention of keeping the other part, losing Estrildis. There were a series of underground passages under London, and at the end of one of these, Locrinus installed his mistress.

To be fair to him, he made the cavern as hospitable as could be managed. He had the walls lime-washed to make it a bit brighter, although the water seeping through the rock soon made them stained; he even had rich furnishings brought down so that it took on the appearance of a room in the royal palace. But nothing could disguise the fact that it was really cold, damp and dark; a dungeon more than a princess' chamber.

People noticed that he was spending an inordinate amount of time underground. He explained that he was honouring the goddess of the place, and taking council from her. He must have thought himself pretty clever for coming up with that one. So he gained a reputation as one who has the ear of the gods; quite an important attribute for a king in those days.

This went on for seven years. Inevitably at some point, Estrildis became pregnant. She gave birth to a girl, who grew up in this strange, dark environment. She had the fair hair of her mother, but having grown up in this place without sun, her skin was pale – almost translucent – and the only human company she knew was that of her mother and the strange man who visited occasionally. Her father would watch her as she played so seriously and thought her like a creature from another world.

At the end of these seven years Corineus died. Locrinus saw his chance to live the life he had always wanted to live. He banished Gwendolen and brought Estrildis up from the depths where she had been hidden, together with the exceptional being that was Sabrina. Perhaps you have seen cows, kept in sheds all winter, at last allowed back into the fields in springtime. Or battery hens, kept in cages all their lives who are suddenly given their freedom. At first they cannot believe it, but then, as they begin to understand their new joy, they run and frolic with the sheer delight of being alive. So imagine how it was for Sabrina. At first she was blinded by the terrible bright light but then, as she slowly discovered how big the world was and how many wonderful things there were in it, she began to explore these wonders with a feverish intensity. Imagine running barefoot on grass for the first time; imagine seeing and smelling a flower, imagine swimming in a wide river. Each day brought something new and exciting until Sabrina thought she must burst with the sheer pleasure of it.

But Gwendolen was her father's daughter. She was not going to just quietly disappear from history. She went to Cornwall and, when the men of Cornwall heard how this daughter of their land had been treated, they were determined on revenge. They sent word to the men of Wales that the Hun, though defeated on the battlefield, had conquered the island through the wiles of the bedroom. The two peoples must unite and march on London to right this wrong.

When news of their plan reached Locrinus, he knew that his kingdom would be lost if the two armies joined. He was determined to march and give battle to the smaller Cornish force before it met the Welsh. As she saw preparations being made, Estrildis went to Locrinus and pleaded with him to take Sabrina and herself with him. 'The army is no place for a princess and her daughter,' he said.

She replied 'without your personal protection, we are dead. Your people have no love for us. They blame us for this war and the deaths that will come from it.'

Locrinus saw the sense of this. 'Come then. We will live together or die together.'

The army set off, but now it seemed that the gods were against them. Every day brought rain. Sabrina loved it, the way it fell on her upturned face, but it did not take long for the roads to become streams of mud, slowing the baggage train to a crawl. Locrinus shouted and cursed but, in the pit of his stomach, he felt the heavy weight of defeat.

Inevitably, word came that the Cornish and Welsh forces had united. Locrinus tried to rally his troops with good humour, but he saw in their eyes that they had already convinced themselves that they had lost. Every morning, fewer men took up their position, as those who had no wish to die for a doomed cause crept away in the dark of night.

The two armies eventually met near the settlement that is now called Stourport-on-Severn. You could not fault Locrinus' bravery, nor that of the men who fought beside him. Knowing that if he was to win at all it must be quickly, he charged into the centre of the enemy, hoping to kill as many chiefs as possible and so weaken his foes' stomach for the fight. But the task was too great, and Locrinus was forced back and then killed. Now the great slaughter began as each man, knowing all was lost, tried to find his own safety.

Estrildis and Sabrina had watched the battle from the rear. When soldiers with fear-mad eyes came running past them, news of Locrinus' death on their lips, she made no attempt to run. What place was there to go to? When fierce men with blood dripping from their spears and swords came for her, she met their eyes until they glanced away; she was a Hunnish princess, and she would fear no one. Sabrina could understand nothing of what was going on but, in all the shouting and screaming, she did not wish for a moment to be back in her safe but dark cave.

They were brought before Gwendolen, who looked upon them with contempt. 'Take them to the river. Drown them. I will not even allow them enough British soil to be buried in.'

So it was done. Estrildis was thrown in first, and she slipped beneath the water without a sound. Then the men grabbed the little creature Sabrina. They did not even bother to tie her hands.

That would be a waste of good rope. For a moment there was a wonderful sense of flying, and then the cold water shocked her into oblivion.

But it is said that the spirits of the place took pity on this innocent child. They accepted her as one of their own. Over the years stories grew up of a river nymph who haunted these waters. Occasionally, especially in the early morning or the dusk of evening, you could feel her presence. She was given many names. Some say she was originally called Habrenna, in Welsh she was known as Hafren and to the Romans she was called by the name we usually know her by, Sabrina. Whenever poets or others romantically inclined persons wished to personify this, the longest river in Britain, they would conjure up the magic of this name.

Geoffrey of Monmouth has, for many hundreds of years, been regarded as a fantasist. Historians are pretty sure that no invasion by the Huns ever took place, nor did any Trojans

found a civilisation in Britain. But, in recent years, scholars have reconsidered this position. Stephen J. Yeates has concluded that Geoffrey's work '… is littered with characters and ideas which are not simply a product of medieval pseudo history, but use longstanding ideas of spirit of place and the names of divinities out of context … Thus, Geoffrey of Monmouth may not have considered himself the originator of his tale … but as the interpreter of a number of older traditions.' (Yeates, p.72)

Just as the Welsh Mabinogion has come down to us as a rather garbled story of heroes that might originally have been myths about the aboriginal British gods, so this story of Sabrina might be a retelling of a retelling of a retelling of a now lost story of a British goddess. Geoffrey retold it in the twelfth century, and now I am retelling it to you in the twenty-first. Better still, you could always sit down on the banks of the Severn one quiet night and see if Habrenna will tell you any more of her story.

THREE

TO MAKE A FIRE

The fire had gone out. None of King Osric's retainers could remember a time when the great fire had not burned in the centre of the king's great hall. It was one of the great sights in the land of the Weorgoran, the sub-kingdom of the Hwicce, who had taken over from the Romans as the rulers of the land we now call Worcestershire.

The fire was used for everything, from cooking the meals for everyone in the household to warming their cold bones after a busy day. If anyone in the royal enclosure wanted a fire, they had only to slip down to the hall and pick up a burning log and they could go off and make their own fire.

But now the fire was out. Worse than that, it was the middle of winter, with a foot of snow outside and some very cold and annoyed people inside. The cook stared at it for ages in disbelief. He looked at the scullion, whose job it was to keep the fire alight through the night, who shrugged and looked at his feet. 'Not my fault. The kindling was wet.'

'So how are we going to relight it?'

No one knew. The fire had never gone out before. A frantic search was made for any fires that still might be lit and could be used to start a blaze, but it soon became apparent that all the other fires had gone out as well.

The cook was still looking despondently at the grey ashes that had once been the great fire, when there was a commotion at one end of the hall; King Osric himself came in, and the cook knew that he would want his porridge.

The cook saw no help for it but to go to the king and explain himself. 'I'm sorry your lordship, but the great fire has gone out, so I can't make your porridge.'

'Gone out! But it's never gone out.'

'It has now.'

'Well, relight it.'

'That's the trouble. Everyone has forgotten how to light a fire.'

'Look, I'm a king. I can't be bothered with things like that. I've got plots to plot and schemes to scheme, important things. I'll have cold venison for breakfast. You sort out the fire.'

The cook went to see the court magician to see if he had any spells to start a fire.

'Of course I haven't,' said the magician, shivering slightly. 'My spells are for important things, not for boring things like fire.'

So the cook went to see the court librarian. He had some really old books in his library. Surely some of those would explain how to set a fire.

The librarian burrowed away amongst the shelves. 'Yes, here it is,' he said. 'You rub two sticks together.'

The cook was dubious; but it was in a book, so it must be so. He went back down to the kitchen, picked up a couple of logs from the pile and started to rub them together.

After fifteen minutes he had certainly got warmer, but there was no sign of any fire. He threw the logs down in disgust.

Just then, there was a commotion at one end of the hall. The king came in, wanting his hot stew.

'I'm sorry your lordship, we still haven't managed to light the fire.'

'For goodness sake! How long can it take?'

'There's just no one in the whole settlement who knows how to do it.'

The king thought for a moment. 'Someone will have to be sent out to bring back a fire.' He looked around the court. 'Where's my good-for-nothing son? He's never done anything in his life. He can go.'

Prince Oswald was sent for, and his mission was explained to him. It was true that he had never done anything useful in his life, but that was mostly because no one had asked him to do anything. He was rather looking forward to the adventure.

He turned to go but his father called him back. 'Haven't you forgotten something?'

The boy looked around but nothing came to mind.

'If you are going to bring back some fire then you are probably going to need something to carry it back in.'

The prince clicked his fingers in enlightenment. There was an old helmet lying on the floor that nobody seemed to be using, so he picked that up and set off.

It was not nearly as much fun as he had expected, trudging through a foot of snow, and he had not realised there was a biting wind. Of all the adventures Oswald had listened to, he could not remember one of them where the hero had been so miserable and cold.

The first house he came to was a large merchant's house. He knocked on the door. When it was opened by a servant, he explained what he wanted and was quickly let in. The merchant

was very happy that the prince had come to his house and
wanted something from him.

'Of course you can have some of my fire. Help yourself.'

Oswald was just about to reach out and pluck a burning
brand when the merchant continued. 'Of course, I am a merchant. We ought to negotiate over price.'

'Yes, I suppose so,' said the prince.

'From what I've heard, it's usual in these circumstances to
pay half the kingdom.'

The prince thought about this. It seemed a trifle expensive for
one piece of wood, but his father wanted a fire and he did not
want to disappoint him. So, agreeing that, if the fire was lit successfully, the merchant was entitled to half the kingdom, he put a
piece of burning wood in the helmet and set off back to the hall.

It started off well, and Oswald thought of how pleased his
father would be when he returned with the fire. But gradually he
realised that his hands were getting hot, and that was because the
helmet was getting hot, and that was because the wood was burning brightly in the helmet. He tried to ignore it but the heat got
stronger and stronger and the pain got worse and worse, no matter
how much he tried to change hands. In the end he could not bear
it anymore and dropped the helmet in the snow. The wood fell
out and the fire was immediately extinguished by the snow.

The prince looked sadly at the charred wood smoking
slightly. He did not relish the idea of returning to the merchant
and explaining what had happened; perhaps this time it would
be the whole of the kingdom. He set off in another direction.

Eventually Oswald came to a cottage at the edge of a forest.
When he knocked on the door, it was opened by a man carrying an axe. But it was all right; the man was a woodcutter, so
had a good reason to be carrying an axe.

Again the prince explained his problem. The woodcutter was very pleased to help, but just as the prince was reaching out to take some of the wood, he gave a little cough.

'You know what? I've got really fed up of this woodcutting. The thing I fancy now is being captain of the guard. Perhaps in return for that burning log you could put in a good word for me.'

Well, it was less than half the kingdom, so the prince thought he had got a good deal. He readily agreed that, if the woodcutter's fire was used to relight the great fire, he would talk to his father about appointing a new captain of the guard. It was only when they shook on it that the prince noticed that the woodcutter had two fingers missing from his left hand. Not the most successful woodcutter then; and the prince wondered just how effective he would be as the captain of the guard. Still, a promise is a promise.

It was as he was about to take a burning log from the woodcutter's fire that he realised that he had left the helmet back in the snow. He had no choice but to pick up the log and carry it in his hand.

This was not so much fun when he was outside in the wind. It was either trying to blow the fire out, or blowing the flames back onto his hand. Eventually the inevitable happened. The wind blew, the flames flew and the prince cried out in pain as they stung his fingers. He dropped the log onto the snow; the flames sputtered, smoked a bit and then went out.

The prince looked at the charred log despondently. Looking on the bright side, Oswald thought that at least now he did not have to explain to the current captain of the guard why an inefficient woodcutter should take over his job.

He took another path into the forest. It was dark in here, and the prince felt that it could not be long before the night set in. He was thankful, then, when he saw a thin column of smoke rising above the trees. It proved to be a small hovel, hardly worthy of the name of dwelling. In the normal course of events Oswald would probably have gone straight past it, but these were not usual times.

He was going to knock on the door but it looked so flimsy that he thought that if he did, he would put his hand straight through it. 'Hello, is anyone there?' he called out.

The door was pulled back and a young woman stood there. It struck the prince that she was more beautiful than most of the young women who lived in his father's hall, but quickly pulling himself together, he explained his problem.

'Of course you can have some fire. Take as much as you want.'

The prince looked at the poor fire in the hearth. It would be difficult to take anything without putting it out completely. And, on past performance, it would be a bit of a waste of time. He would probably only drop it on the way.

'Is something the matter?' the girl asked.

Oswald explained his bad luck that day.

'Look, I've got my flint and tinder box. Why don't I come back with you and make the fire at the palace?'

Oswald thought this was a wonderful idea. The girl gathered her fire making implements together and they set off. By this time it was starting to get dark, and although he was a prince and therefore very brave, he was quite glad to have the young woman with him.

Eventually they arrived back at the palace. Everyone stood around, amazed, at the ease with which the girl made a ball of the tinder, flashed a spark from her flint onto it and blew until the fire was alight.

'You better watch well,' she said, 'so that you can all do it yourselves next time.'

The king was so pleased to have warmth again that he ordered a feast to be prepared, and the girl was invited, although she just wanted to go home.

As the prince sat in the warm hall with the warm food inside him, listening to the strange tales of the storytellers, he began to think. You know, all the others wanted something from me, but she did not ask for anything. In fact she came all this way back with me. Oswald looked over at her and thought she looked very well in the candlelight. Then he turned to the king. 'Father, don't you think it's time I was married?'

FOUR

ST EGWIN

Being born in the seventh century was tough for anyone. However, if you had been given a choice, being born into the royal house of Mercia was probably one of the better ones.

Such was Egwin's fate. Unfortunately he was not happy with it. He was not an athletic boy, and hated being made to practice with shield, spear and sword every day so that he would be ready to take his place at the front of the shield wall when he was older, as was his privilege as a prince of the royal blood. He much preferred listening to the monk who was his tutor as he talked about Christ and the saints. In his daydreams he performed miracles instead of daring deeds of arms.

When he reached fourteen, his father accepted the inevitable. His bodyguard told him that Egwin would be a liability in war, so little did he have any inclination for the use of arms, and they had no intention of standing anywhere near him in a battle. So Egwin was given as a novice to the local monastery. At first he liked the strict timetable and constant prayer and devotion, but as he grew older, he started to find this regime too confining. Life in the monastery was too easy, with regular food and a warm bed. He determined to leave and become a hermit. Since his strict nature made him unpopular with the other monks, the abbot agreed that this would be a good idea.

Egwin went off into the wilds of Worcestershire, which were easier to find in those days, and lived in seclusion, contemplating the mystery of God.

But the people of Worcestershire would not leave him alone. Naturally he acquired a reputation for holiness, so crowds would flock to see him, be touched by him or listen to what he had to say. It was all very trying, because all Egwin wanted to do was be quiet and think about God; but he knew that it was his Christian duty to minister to the poor, so he did his best to put up with it.

Then something worse happened. Bishop Oftfor, the second bishop of Worcester, died; it was generally felt that Egwin was the best person to take his place. His brother (now King Ethelred of Mercia) certainly thought so, because it would be very useful to have a close relation as a bishop, but Egwin was horrified. A bishop had many duties, constantly touring his diocese and ensuring that this still new religion was being followed correctly. However, Archbishop Brithwold assured him that there was no better candidate, and King Ethelred told him it was about time he did something for the family. Reluctantly Egwin accepted.

As he feared, being a bishop was a terrible job. He never had any time for himself because everyone came to him with problems or requests. He even had a swineherd called Eof asking to see him, because the fellow was having visions of Our Lady. It was not the business of swineherds to have visions; even Egwin had never had a vision. If the people had chosen him, he was going to make them suffer for it. Oftfor had been a bit too lax for his liking. It was time to get the place in order. The people of Worcestershire must put aside their semi-pagan ways and start getting used to the restraints of Christian morality. He belaboured his flock on the sanctity of marriage; none of this wandering off into the forest when the fancy took them. They must observe the days of fasting, conform to ecclesiastical doctrine, and above all, NO BOOZING!

Soon people were wondering what they had done in letting this righteous monster become bishop. Muttering became resentment, and resentment became discussion on how bishops could be done away with. Then Egwin made his biggest mistake: he started reminding his clerics about the importance of chastity among the priesthood. Nothing could be better guaranteed to get him into trouble, because priests could write and they could write to the Pope in Rome, describing in cruel detail how Egwin's intransigence was driving people back to the old religion.

A letter came, demanding that Egwin make a pilgrimage to Rome to answer for his faults. Egwin was incensed. The ungrateful people had made him bishop and then, when he had tried to do a good job, blackened his name and attempted to get rid of him.

Even today it is not the easiest thing to get to Rome, as anyone who has travelled by Alitalia knows. Egwin would have to make the journey on foot, and it would be a long and dangerous expedition. Even so, there were a few who believed in Egwin and volunteered to go with him. However, Egwin was not satisfied with just having to walk halfway across the known world. At a place called Hurdingpool he summoned a blacksmith and made the man put fetters on his legs and lock them so that he could go to the Pope the way Our Lord had gone to Pilate. Then he shuffled towards the banks of the Avon and threw the key into the river. He gazed at his accusers with a look on his face that said, 'There, now look what you've made me do.'

'Now these shackles will stay on my legs until God proves me innocent!' With a flounce he turned round and set off for Rome. It was a long and difficult journey. Most of the people they met assumed Egwin was a terrible criminal, and wanted to throw something at him. His companions had to spend most of their time explaining the situation. He had made their life much more difficult.

At last the group reached Rome and waited for Egwin's meeting with the Pope. Now, if a bishop's life is busy, how much more so is that of the head of the Church? Day after day the group from Worcestershire were forced to wait. One day Egwin went off to pray at the tomb of St Peter, leaving his companions at a loose end.

The youngest of the party looked over the bridge at the brown waters of the Tiber flowing beneath them. 'Why don't we try fishing?' he said. 'It will remind us of our own dear Avon, although it is so many miles away, and it might provide something for our evening meal.'

They fashioned together a rod and line and found some worms, and soon they were fishing almost as merrily as if they were back at their own native river. Passers-by laughed to see these foreign monks who thought they could catch anything in those polluted waters.

Suddenly the monk whose turn it was to have the rod gave a shout. Something had taken the bait. Ignoring the advice coming from his fellows, he waited until he was sure and then pulled the fish up onto the parapet. It was a fine-looking salmon, and at the sight of it, they remembered how hungry they were. While the rest of the monks went to look for the makings of a fire, the one who had caught it set to gutting it and preparing it for cooking. Suddenly he let out a cry. As his companions turned around to look, he lifted up a large key that he had found in the fish's stomach.

'Surely that is the key that Bishop Egwin threw into the Avon!' exclaimed one.

'That's impossible,' said another.

'Well, there's only one way to find out,' cried a third.

They rushed to the tomb of St Peter and found Egwin still praying. At first he was annoyed at being disturbed, but when they told their story and showed him the key, he too was over-awed. With trembling hands one of the monks fitted the key into the lock. There was a click, and the shackles fell off.

News of the miracle spread throughout Rome, and the next day, Egwin and his monks were summoned to an audience with the Pope where they again told the story, and showed the Pope the fetters and the key, although the fish was by now absent, having been eaten the previous evening. The Pope was duly impressed and declared it a sign from God that proved Egwin's innocence. Egwin returned to Worcester much faster than he had set out, armed with a letter from the Holy Father declaring his complete faith in the bishop. His accusers' plan had blown up in their faces.

But Egwin had learned some humility on his travels. When Eof next came to see him to tell him about his visions, Egwin listened. Eof told him that he had been sitting on the banks of the Avon, at Hurdingpool, where Egwin had thrown the key into the river. It was very peaceful and it seemed to Eof that he could hear beautiful music. Suddenly the mist over the river coalesced into a woman of surpassing beauty, dressed in a blue the colour of the summer sky, flanked by two others whose robes seemed to shimmer like silver in sunlight. But it was the smile on the lady's face that Eof most remembered; a smile of such compassion and joy that it felt to Eof that he was already in heaven.

Now Egwin and Eof went together to that spot, along with Egwin's faithful monks. They sang psalms, they prayed and they waited. At last they too heard the ethereal music, but it was Egwin who now saw the lady and her companions gliding over the water. Now he looked into her face and felt peace that he had never felt before. He had been granted a vision as well as a miracle, but it would be the vision and the look of serenity he had seen on the face of the Mother of Our Lord herself that remained the most important thing to him.

Egwin ordered that an abbey be built on the spot, dedicated to the Blessed Virgin. Eventually, a few centuries later, it was also dedicated to St Egwin. Because of the favour in which the Pope held Egwin it was granted many favours and reductions in dues so that became a large and impressive building. The area is still called Eof's place, Eof's ham, Evesham.

LEGENDS OF WORCESTER CATHEDRAL

The first bishop of Worcester was named Bosel, and the See was founded in around 680; its boundaries, as was the normal pattern, reflecting the boundaries of the local tribe. In this case it was the Hwicce.

The first actual cathedral appears to have been built by Bishop Oswald in around 961. Most buildings, even the important ones at this period, were built of timber. However, Oswald determined that Worcester Cathedral should be built of stone, like the churches in Rome.

He therefore had to import Italian masons, who were pretty expensive, and they had to find and quarry suitable stone, which also greatly added to the bill. People shook their heads and said that no good would come of it, and even some of Oswald's fellow clergy began to wonder if he was the right man for the job.

Things got worse when the masons had prepared the first stone, and were getting ready to transport it to the chosen site near the Severn. They found they could not move it, whatever means they tried. Even a gang of eighty men and oxen could not get it to budge. When word of this got out, people decided that the masons Oswald had chosen must be incompetent and Oswald himself a naive fool.

In desperation, Oswald himself went to the quarry to see what the matter was. With his saintly eye he saw that there was a small devil sitting on the block, grinning malevolently. When the imp realised the bishop could see him and was about to put a godly blessing on the stone, he let out a terrible shriek and a sulphurous stench, and disappeared in a flash of blue lightning. Now the block of stone could be moved as easily as if it was on rollers. Once it was realised that Oswald was such a holy man that he could command devils, all the whispering behind his back stopped, and very soon after his death, he was proclaimed St Oswald.

Soon after this time, there was yet another round of Viking raids. On this particular occasion some of King Ethelred's advisers came up with the idea that if they paid the raiders to go away, life would be easier for everybody. Unfortunately they had to get the money from somewhere, and the only way they could do that was by putting up taxes, which did not make them very popular. The other problem with the plan was that the next raiding season the Danes came back saying that, unfortunately, they had spent last year's money, so could they have some more please. Otherwise they would be forced to go back to pillaging.

So it went on for several years until Ethelred had become so unpopular that the Danish king, Sweyn Forkbeard, decided that he had a good chance of becoming King of the English in Ethelred's place and got together a war band strong enough for an actual invasion. He was right in his expectation; Ethelred had lost all support and was soon dead. Sweyn became king and married Ethelred's queen, Emma of Normandy.

Unfortunately for the English, Sweyn saw no reason not to continue collecting the taxes and this continued under Sweyn's son, Cnut. It got no better under Cnut's son, Harthacnut. The people of Worcester particularly resented this taxation, having been sufficiently distant from Danish raiders that they did not see any reason for paying them off in the first place. It was particularly unfortunate then that, in 1041, Harthacnut chose to send the most arrogant of his nobles to collect the taxes from Worcester; a man who despised the English, and was not going to placate them in any way, or be careful not to tread on their sensibilities.

As the man shouted and swore, determined to extract the most tribute he could, the tension in the town grew until the cauldron was close to boiling. No one knew who threw the first stone, but it caught the Dane on the side of the cheek and drew blood. He became even angrier but it also broke some restraint within the crowd, seeing that the man could be injured. Even a noble, however battle-trained, cannot hold off a mob for long and he was soon beaten senseless. But the mob had not finished with him yet; they were determined to literally do to him what they thought he had metaphorically done to them – flay the skin off their backs.

They fetched a butcher, who had the necessary skills. He stripped the wretch's clothes off, and then proceeded to strip the skin off his body. Whether the fellow was alive at this juncture is a moot point, because he certainly was not at the end of the process. The carcass they threw into the River Severn, but the skin was tanned and nailed to the inside of the great west door of the cathedral, as a dreadful warning to anyone else not to take the people of Worcester lightly.

However, the Dane's entourage had seen how the wind was blowing much faster than their master, and had ridden for their lives when the unpleasantness started. They rode straight to Harthacnut's court in Winchester. Naturally the king was incensed when he heard what had happened to his retainer and that the taxes had not been collected. He sent raiders to burn Worcester to the ground, which they did very successfully. However, one of the populace had the foresight to take the Dane's skin down from the door before they arrived, rightly thinking that the sight might annoy them even more.

A few months later, Harthacnut died, and the Saxon Edward was able to take the throne. The Dane's skin was brought back to its place of honour on the cathedral door, and there it remained for many centuries, for the amusement or horror of visitors. It was only in the middle of the nineteenth century that the exhibit was considered too gruesome for modern sensibilities and permanently removed. At the same time, the opportunity was taken for scientific analysis and it was found to be definitely human.

However, a later examination, using more powerful instruments in the twentieth century, concluded that it was probably the skin of a pig.

****

A few years into King Edward's reign, Wulstan was appointed bishop. He was a keen social reformer, especially angered by the slave trade that was flourishing in the area. He was so successful that he even managed to stop the slave trade in Bristol, at least for several centuries. Despite being a close friend and adviser to Harold Godwinnson, Duke William uniquely allowed him to remain bishop after 1066, such was his reputation for pastoral care. When he died it was considered only fitting to declare him a saint, the third bishop of Worcester to get such a promotion.

Although King John is often considered one of the worst kings in English history, he had a soft spot for Worcester Cathedral. So much so that, when he died, he left orders that he was to be buried there. Not just that, but he specified that his tomb should be between those of St Oswald and St Wulstan and that he was to be buried in the habit of a monk. Presumably he hoped that, come the Last Judgement, being so apparelled and in such august company, God would go easy on him. Only time will tell if he has been successful in this.

Another illustrious person to be buried in Worcester Cathedral is Arthur, son of Henry VII. It is said that because his brother is buried here, Henry VIII was more lenient to the Worcester monks than he was to other establishments at the time of the Dissolution of the Monasteries.

Six

Brihtric Meaw

Many people envied Brihtric, son of Algar, the Lord of Gloucester. He was nicknamed Meaw (Snow) because of the fairness of his complexion, which would make many young women turn their heads, he stood to inherit his father's large estates in Worcestershire and Gloucestershire; and worse, he was an extremely pious and serious young man who, despite his wealth, never caused his father any anxiety about his behaviour or the company he kept.

When Brihtric was twenty-two years of age, his father decided that he should learn more of the world. He went to see his friend King Edward, and asked if there was any employment that he could find for his son. The king had a think about it and then nodded.

'I am in negotiation with Baldwin, Count of Flanders,' he said. 'The Count is a fair man, and the treaty of friendship should be an easy thing to sort out. I will send your son to complete the final arrangements.'

Algar was pleased with this and rushed to tell his son, who was also quite pleased at the opportunity to serve his king. So, a few days later, he crossed the channel in a small boat (the only way of doing it at that time); not the most pleasant way to spend your day. He headed for Lille, where the Count of Flanders was holding court.

He was welcomed with all the dignity befitting the emissary of the King of England. A feast was held in his honour and he was seated between the Count and his young daughter, Matilda. Throughout the festivities Brihtric became conscious that Matilda could not take her eyes off him. Every mouthful of food he took, every drop of wine he drank, she was watching it. At first he smiled back at her but, as the meal progressed, he started feeling irritated and not a little annoyed.

The next day he was locked in close discussions with Baldwin. It was not difficult work, just a little over-meticulous for his liking. It was a bright, sunny day, and for all his seriousness, Brihtric would have preferred being out in the fresh air rather than in the dark, smoky hall. At last, business was over and Brihtric lost no time in getting out of the hall and into the sunshine; but he was a little disconcerted when he found Matilda lurking outside, as if she had been waiting for him.

'Have you finished your business with father?'

Not without a little irritation Brihtric gazed down at her. 'I have,' he consented.

'Then perhaps you'd like to come up to my chamber and have a look at my tapestries. People say I'm really good at needlework.'

'My lady, I think it would be rather improper, even for someone of such tender years such as yourself, to allow a young man into your private rooms.'

'What do you mean?'

Brihtric felt the air around him change but he did not understand why. 'Well, dear little Matilda, although you are only, what, twelve … ?'

He saw her face break from a smile into burning rage. 'I'm twenty-one!' she bellowed, and then stormed off. What no one had thought to tell him was that the count's daughter was vertically challenged. Now he had created a diplomatic incident.

He rushed to apologise to her father, but Baldwin bellowed with laughter. 'Don't worry about it, young man. Matilda's got a thick skin. Has to have, if she's going to survive in this court. She'll get over it. You'll see at dinner that it has all blown over.'

Brihtric was concerned when he found that he was again sitting next to Matilda at the meal, although it seemed to be just as Baldwin had said. She behaved as if nothing untoward had happened, but was still attentive towards him. It seemed she was still watching his every move. What had been annoying coming from a small girl was deeply disturbing to Brihtric when it came from a young woman only a year younger than him.

At one stage she stabbed a piece of meat that was on his plate and then ate it in a very unseemly fashion. Even more provocatively, she then took another piece that had been on her plate and held it up to him, as if he was a dog who was supposed to beg for it. He tried to ignore her.

'Don't worry, dear Brihtric. My father would not object if you paid court to me. Although you are not a ruler, you are of noble blood, and with fine estates, I hear. We would make a good marriage.'

Brihtric was appalled. 'Madam, in my country it is not done for women to be so forward, lest they be mistaken for a strumpet.'

For a moment Brihtric thought Matilda was going to throw her cup of wine over him, and she certainly looked as if she was considering it. Eventually she managed to control herself, and was content with storming out of the hall. Everyone looked at

Brihtric who blushed as brightly as a bullfinch. The following day, he made his excuses and left. As he put his foot on the ship that would take him home he breathed a sigh of relief, thinking all that unpleasantness was behind him. He could not have been more wrong.

Matilda, meanwhile, felt that her heart was broken. Her father was quite anxious to get her off his hands; but now she would not countenance any other suitor, though, with the lands that would come with her, there were quite a few of those. One of the most prominent was William, Duke of Normandy. When Matilda heard that, she let out a terrible yowl: 'I will never marry a bastard!'

That word got back to Duke William. It was well-known that he was the result of a liaison between his father, the previous duke, and a tanner's daughter. His illegitimacy was a very sore point with him, and he was not the sort of man to take this lightly.

With only a few of his bodyguards, he rode to Lille and waited for Matilda in the town square as she came from Mass. As she approached he walked up to her, and without saying a word, cuffed her on the head, which sent her sprawling in the mud and set her maids to screaming. Then he was quickly on his horse and away, before Baldwin's soldiers knew what was happening.

Naturally such an affront cannot go unpunished. The Count of Flanders took his army and burned some Norman villages, and killed a few peasants who did not get out of the way in time. Such a thing could not go unpunished so William burnt some Flemish villages and killed a few peasants. After honour being satisfied on both sides, a peace treaty was signed; one of the clauses was that Matilda would marry William.

Whether Baldwin had got his daughter to see sense, or Matilda had decided that William must be really serious about the match, we do not know.

Then, in 1066, King Edward of England died, having (according to Duke William) promised the throne to him. Earl Harold Godwinnson declared himself the rightful English king; William invaded and the two armies met at Hastings. The rest, as they say, is history.

This did not worry Brihtric. When news came of the battle, and that all who had fought at Hastings or who had supported Harold would forfeit their land, he felt no cause for concern. He had been loyal to Edward; believed that William had been Edward's heir; and had no love for the Godwinnsons, thinking them troublesome and brutal.

He had other things on his mind. He had just completed a new chapel at his holding in Hanley, and had invited the saintly Bishop Wulfstan of Worcester to dedicate it. The festivities had been lavish, befitting such a mighty landholder. The feast at the end of the day's celebrations had just begun when armed and mailed Norman knights broke into the hall. At their head was Roger fitz-Hamon, one of William's most trusted followers. No man of Brihtric's was armed; they had left their swords outside, as was proper at a feast, so could do nothing to prevent fitz-Hamon seizing Brithric and dragging him out of the hall.

He was forced to mount a horse and the party rode to Winchester, where William had installed his court. When they reached it, Brihtric, without trial or further ceremony, was thrown into a dungeon and left to rot. He was dead within weeks.

The chroniclers are divided as to whether this was the work of Matilda, getting her revenge, or the work of William, getting rid of the man who had first stolen his wife's heart. Certainly Matilda got most of Brihtric's land but William was suspicious of Saxon lords, if they had supported Harold or not, and by 1086, the time of Domesday Book, had replaced most of them.

Historians are also divided on William and Matilda's marriage. Some say she was a great help to William, taking care of day to day affairs while he was off campaigning, and being the first consort of an English king to be awarded the title Queen. Others say she led him a merry dance, encouraged his sons to rebel against him and never forgave him for not being her first love, Brihtric Meaw.

SEVEN

ROBIN OF HORSEHILL

The Norman invaders were not, on the whole, pleasing to look at. Thick upper bodies from all that knightly training, pugnacious faces with short cropped hair; they would not have looked out of place in a professional rugby team.

Fortunately, some of their women-folk were better looking and Honoria, daughter of the lord of Tickenhill, was considered better than most. So much so, that all the young knights and squires and even some of the nobility dreamed that they would take her as their bride, and also take control of the substantial tracts of land that came with her.

But Honoria's heart was elsewhere. She loved Robin of Horsehill, and he loved her in return. They had known each other since childhood, but Robin was only a poor knight's son. He would bring no land or wealth to the marriage, and they both knew that the ambitious lord of Tickenhill would never countenance the match. Honoria was his only daughter, his wife having died; he had no inclination to find another. So all his hopes rested on Honoria, and he was determined she should have the richest husband he could find for her.

The only remembrance Honoria had of her mother was a silver ring, which she wore constantly. Naturally she was very fond of it as, secretly, was her father. For all his bluff and bluster he had loved his wife, as he loved his daughter. He would often sit in the evenings and quietly look at the ring glinting on his daughter's finger and feel a little melancholy.

One hot spring day Honoria went boating on the Severn, accompanied by her nurse and a servant to do the actual rowing. It was cooler on the river than at the manor, and Honoria could not resist trailing her hand in the cold water. Suddenly she let out a scream. 'My ring! It's gone!'

The servant stopped rowing and the nurse dropped her embroidery. Honoria leaned over to see if she could see the ring on the river bed, but that only made the nurse start screaming because she thought the boat would turn over. The servant, fearing it would be him who would get into trouble, jumped into the water and started scrabbling about but only succeeded in stirring up all the mud and making the nurse have hysterics because she feared the boat would be swept away right down to the sea.

There was no help for it but to go back to Tickenhill, and for Honoria to explain to her father what had happened. He did what you would do – he went absolutely mad. Not only was he annoyed that his child had been stupid; he had also lost a connection with the woman that he had loved.

'You have let me down, Honoria. How could you be so careless? You need taking in hand. You shall marry whoever finds your ring, be he knight or villein. Perhaps he will be able to teach you some sense.'

Now we all say things we regret in the heat of the moment, but before he had time to take them back, Honoria burst into tears and ran out of the hall. So the words were said, and no gentleman can go back on his word and keep his honour.

The news caused excitement throughout the county. The next morning all the young knights and squires who dreamed of a manor of their own, which was just about all of them, went wading in the Severn, hoping to find the ring. Naturally, all they did was turn the river brown as they stirred up the river bed.

Robin of Horsehill did not join them. How would you feel if all these idiots were attempting to marry your beloved? Robin was depressed and broken-hearted. Instead, in one of those self-destructive gestures that young men are quite capable of, he went off hunting.

He went hunting at Blackingstone Rock, just north-west of Stourport. He and Honoria had sometimes come here. She had said it was one of her favourite spots. She used to say that this place felt special, as if it was sacred in some way; that if ever things went wrong in her life, this was the place she would want to come and hide. Some said that it was near this spot that Sabrina was thrown into the river. Robin had rather hoped that Honoria might have come here after the terrible things that had happened. There was no sign of her however, so he crept silently through the wood, waiting for a suitable quarry to present itself.

When he could see the tower of Ribbesford Church on the other bank of the Severn, he stopped and waited. This, he knew, was a favourite watering spot, where the deer came down to drink. The wind was in the right direction; anything coming to the river back would not scent him. He just had to remain still and wait. It was a dangerous thing to do – he had no licence to hunt deer from the king, but he did not care about that anymore.

Sure enough, within half an hour, he saw movement in the bushes on the other side of the river, and a fallow doe came out of cover. Nervously, she looked around and smelled the air. Robin remained absolutely still. At last, the doe approached the dip in the bank where she could get down to the water and drink. With almost imperceptible movement, Robin raised his bow with the arrow already nocked. Quietly he breathed in and steadied himself. Then he loosed the arrow.

The moment he did so, a salmon leapt out of the water. The splash and the movement set the deer running off, but the arrow caught the salmon cleanly and carried it over to the river bank where it lay, flapping its tail, with the arrow sticking out of it.

Robin laughed. It seemed nothing was going his way. He had exchanged a deer for a salmon. Ah well, supper was supper. He waded across the stream to retrieve it. At least no one could hang him for taking a salmon.

With wet feet he walked back home and gave the salmon to one of his servants to prepare. The hunting expedition had done nothing to lighten his mood. If anything, he was even more despondent. When he came back into the hall, he found his servant waiting for him, holding the salmon. 'Sir, you should see this.'

He held the salmon open and there, in the fish's stomach, was Honoria's silver ring.

Robin wasted no time, but immediately called for a horse and rode for Tickenhill. Dusk was already falling, and a more sober man might have waited for the following day; but Robin was drunk on joy, and wanted to tell Honoria the good news as soon as possible. Also, he thought it best to hold her father to his bargain before the idea cooled and he thought better of it.

Even so, riding in the twilight is no safe matter and, although Robin wanted to gallop as fast as the horse could take him, he had no wish to ride into a tree and break his neck, so he took it as carefully as a young man in love can take it.

So it was fully dark by the time he arrived at Tickenhill, and he had some trouble getting past the guards, but eventually he made them understand that his mission was urgent. Honoria looked delighted to see him, her father less so. 'What brings you out so late?'

In answer Robin held up the ring so that it glinted in the candlelight. 'Is this the ring you lost, my lady?'

Honoria laughed with delight. 'Why, yes it is!'

Robin placed it on her finger. 'And do you keep to your promise, my lord?'

The lord of Tickenhill could think of many things to say on that point, but he contented himself with nodding. 'Very well, let it be so.'

So Robin and Honoria were wed, and people came from miles around to help them celebrate. There might have been a few people at the back of the hall who muttered about it all being a put-up job, but what if it was? After all, the salmon of wisdom is a useful ally when you want to marry your true love.

Eight

The Return of
the Crusader

The Crusades brought those of us in Europe better music, more spices to put in our food and access to a lot of the scientific knowledge that we had managed to mislay in the Dark Ages. It also brought death to thousands and misery to millions.

Sir John Attwood was a knight who held land at Wolverley near Kidderminster. Although the great wave of Crusades was over, Sir John was still moved by the idea of fighting for Christ. When news came that a new crusade was being planned, he was determined to join it, despite his wife's pleas and the demands of his lands.

There was a tearful parting when Sir John took leave of his lady, departing for an uncertain future. Sir John took from his hand a large gold ring, unsheathed his sword and cut the ring in two. One half he gave to his wife, and the other he slipped into his purse.

'Take this, my lady; I will keep the other half, and it will be my most dear possession in all my wanderings. When I look upon it, I will think of you and my determination to return to you with honour.'

Then he ruffled the head of his faithful deer hound, a dog that he had looked after since it had been a pup, jumped onto

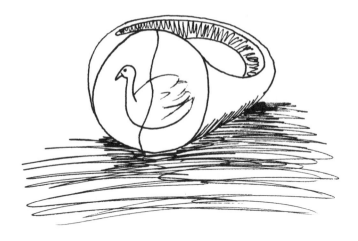

his horse and rode quickly away, his eyes hot with tears and his heart bursting with sadness.

After her lord had left, Lady Attwood was kept busy administering the Attwood estate, but in the evenings, when she had time to be alone in her solar, she would take out the half-ring that now hung by a cord around her neck and gaze at it longingly, hoping the other half would act as a charm to protect her husband and would give him some comfort, even though she often dropped sad tears on her own portion. Then she would ruffle the head of the deer hound, who looked up at her with melancholy eyes, as if asking her when his master would return.

A year passed and news came of great victories that the crusaders had won over the Saracens. This brought her no comfort, because she knew that there would be deaths on both sides in a battle. Another year went by, and now the news was of defeats and loss. Fear gripped her, because her husband had once told her that most deaths occur in an army when it turns and flees. Then the news came that the crusaders were returning.

Although they had little to show for their trouble, this filled her with hope because now, surely, Sir John would return.

But still she waited. At first she looked for him every day, but he did not come. She told herself that he must be delayed on some business, but as the years continued to pass, a deep grief grew inside her and she feared she would never see her husband again.

Five years had passed since Sir John Attwood had set out for the Holy Land. There was talk that she should remarry, since if the family had no heir, the land would revert to the king, and many thought he had enough land already. She knew she had to reconcile herself to being a widow, but the thought of taking another man to her bed filled her with horror. But time raced on, and a nearby lord started paying court to her, suggesting that life would be better under his protection and that it was her duty to add to the race of gentlemen. Given the same counsel from all sides, she eventually consented to the lord's advances, agreeing to marry him on a particular date, a day that meant nothing to him but meant a great deal to her. It would be the sixth anniversary of Sir John's departure. It would be her final act of homage to the man she had loved.

On the early morning of the eve of the wedding, a servant girl went into the fields to milk the house cows. She took with her the deerhound, who would otherwise mope about the place. Still half-asleep, she was surprised when the dog shook off its usual torpor and started barking excitedly. Suddenly it ran off, and she saw it head for what looked like a bundle of rags lying in the field. As the dog ran up, the rags moved and she saw that it was a man.

She was fearful for herself, but also concerned that the dog might savage the man who was probably just some poor soul down on his luck. But, to her surprise, she saw the hound excit-

edly lick the man's face and hands, and the man laugh and
stroke the dog's back. Then she saw that the figure was chained
by the hands.

Now she was really frightened, and ran back to the safety
of the castle. The guard was alerted, and someone went to tell
Lady Attwood. She was determined to see this strange sight for
herself and, accompanied by the girl and a man-at-arms, she
went out to where the dog and the man were still playing with
each other.

'Who are you and what are you doing on my land?' she called
as they approached. The man gave a start and blinked as if he
was still not accustomed to the light. 'Don't you recognise me?'
His voice was barely a croak. His hair was long, matted and
grey, his face lined, his beard long and lousy, and his rags would
have disgraced the poorest beggar in England. But there was
something in that voice that made her head swim, and she felt
that she was going to faint.

'It is me, your husband, the poor creature that was once
Sir John Attwood,' the voice rasped. 'Though I know I am piti-
able and much changed, see, my dog still knows me. And I have
further proof.'

The man reached inside what remained of his tunic.
The man-at-arms instantly drew his sword in case this was
some trick, but the man only pulled out a cord from around
his neck, on which was tied half of a gold ring. The lady's hand
moved to her own neck, and the cord around that. She took it,
and with a shaking hand, gave it to the man. He put the two
pieces together and they fitted perfectly.

With a great cry Lady Attwood ran to Sir John and embraced
him. Tears fell from both their eyes, as they did from the man-
at-arms. The dog barked and wagged his tail.

Sir John was too weak to walk to the castle, so men were sent for to carry him there. By then, news of the miracle had spread and all the staff came to see and then to cheer. Under his lady's nervous supervision, his fetters were cut off, his rags were stripped off him, he was bathed, his hair and beard trimmed. Then he was clothed in vestments befitting a knight, and helped to the great hall where he tucked into a venison stew and some greatly diluted wine. He ate as if he had not eaten properly since he had left six years before, which made his wife sad to see him in such a condition.

At last he was in a fit state to be able to tell them his story. 'Many's the day over the last six years when I've bitterly regretted leaving my beloved Worcestershire, my dear wife and you, my people,' he said; there was not a dry eye in the hall. His wife clasped his hand as if she would never let it go.

'Little did I do to free the Holy Land from the Saracens. In my first battle I was captured and thrown into a dark dungeon. They are heathens and care nothing for ransoms, but preferred to let me rot there. I lost count of how long it was, though now, when you tell me it was six years, it seems a lifetime but also a nightmare that could have been but a day. Yet it was certainly long enough for me to shrivel to the thing you see before you now. One night, when I felt I could endure it no longer, I prayed to God to free me from the living hell with which I was tormented. I have never prayed so fiercely or for so long, and it seemed as if my very soul was leaving my body. I felt joy, thinking the merciful Lord was granting my request in painless death, but then I felt enveloped in this glorious light that lifted me up. The stone walls of my hated prison seemed to fall away, and it was like I was flying through the air, held by this light that felt as soft as feathers.

The next thing I remember was lying on the dear, damp grass of Worcestershire with my own dog licking my face.'

They listened to him in amazement. 'It was an angel that saved you,' said his wife, but Sir John thought of all those bitter years in captivity.

'No, I am not worthy of an angel,' he said. 'I think it was more like a swan.'

Just then the local priest arrived. He had been told of Sir John's miraculous return, but also had more pressing news. A great stone had somehow been dislodged from the tower of his church, and was now lying by the door. If it had happened when he was coming out after saying Mass, he would have been killed. Fortunately, it must have happened in the night. The people listened to him, and all of them thought of Sir John and his unusual homecoming. They had no doubt that the angel that carried Sir John had dislodged the stone in its flight.

You can be sure that Sir John took care never to go too far from Wolverley after that. To commemorate the events, he took a swan for his crest for his great helm, and this can still be seen on the signet rings of Attwoods to this day.

But even a man who has had such adventures cannot put off death forever. When his time came, he was buried in St John's church, under a fine stone effigy. At his feet sat a statue of his faithful hound. Above the tomb were hung the fetters in which he had returned from the Holy Land. One of his fields was set aside in perpetuity, to provide income for a man whose job it was to keep the fetters polished, as an inspiration to all who saw them.

When the church was remodelled in the eighteenth century, the tomb was retained, although the fetters were somehow mislaid. At nearby Wolverley Hall there are some chains that some say are those original fetters, though cynics say they are of more modern manufacture. But what do they know?

NINE

THE BROKEN PEEL

Fairies are often called Pharisees in Worcestershire. This is not, as some ignorant people maintain, down to confusion with the Pharisees of the New Testament, but a dialect double plural, *fairies-s*, because there are a lot of them.

According to Jabez Allies, who wrote *On the Ancient British, Roman and Saxon Antiquities and Folk-Lore of Worcestershire* back in the nineteenth century, Worcester fairies are small and hard-working, ready to help their neighbours and accept help from them, in contrast to some fairies in other parts of the country. Perhaps the reason for their good nature can be found in the following story.

Back in the days before machines had broken our connection to the land, a ploughman and his assistant were ploughing a field with a team of oxen. Matthew, the ploughman, was making sure that the plough dug deep into the hard Cropthorne clay, and Geoffrey was doing his best to keep the team straight.

It was hard work, and both knew that their master would expect them to have ploughed up the acre field by the end of the day.

They were right in the middle of the field, intent on their work, when Matthew thought he heard a strange noise that seemed to be coming from the earth beneath his feet.

'Whoa!' he called to Geoffrey.

'What's the matter?' called Geoffrey, who wanted the work done as quickly as possible.

'Hush a minute,' said Matthew and they both were quiet, listening to the wind in the nearby trees. Geoffrey was just getting impatient when they both heard what sounded like a female voice, crying out in lamentation, 'Oh, what shall I do? I've broken my peel.'

Now, Worcestershire men are noted for their gallantry and determination to help damsels in distress. Without thinking he called out, 'Bring 'un here, missis, and I'll mend 'un.'

Geoffrey was horrified. 'What are you doing? You know what Father Roger has told us about communicating with creatures of Satan.'

'I'll not see anyone in trouble, whoever they are,' said Matthew, who also had more than his fair share of pig-headedness.

The voice had gone quiet, so there was nothing to do but carry on with the ploughing. But, when they approached the headland, Geoffrey stopped suddenly, as if he had been bewitched. 'What's the matter?' cried Matthew, but all Geoffrey could do was point at the bank ahead of him.

Cursing, Matthew made sure the plough was safe and then went to look at what had caused Geoffrey such horror. There on the bank was what looked like a beautifully made child's peel, the long-handled shovel by which loaves can be put in and taken out of the oven. Matthew could see that it was a finely made piece, although the handle was broken in two. He picked it up and examined it. 'Yes, I should be able to do something about this.'

'If you want my advice you wouldn't have anything to do with it.'

'Well, I don't. You've always been a bit too fearful of what Father Roger and his like tells you. Stops you thinking for yourself.'

There was a certain coolness between the two workmates for the rest of the day, but they finished their task in good time and it was still light when Matthew got back to his hut, so he was able to make repairs to the peel. He reckoned it was not the best woodwork he had done, but the peel would be strong enough to do its job. The following day, he went back to the field and left it at the place where it had been found.

All that day Matthew and Geoffrey worked hard ploughing another field, but when that work was finished, Matthew said he was going to see if the peel was still there, although Geoffrey advised against it and would not come with him. When Matthew got to the spot, sure enough, the peel had gone and in its place was a small cake, of a kind he had never seen before. He took it back to show Geoffrey. 'Do you want a bit?'

Geoffrey made the sign of the cross. 'Are you mad? Eat fairy food and you'll be lost forever.'

Matthew looked at Geoffrey as if he was some kind of simpleton that he had not seen before. 'It was a gift. I can't see that it would do me any harm.'

He took a bite. He had never tasted anything so wonderful. For a man who lived mostly on barley stew, it was the sweetest thing he could imagine. As he swallowed the crumbs he could feel the sweetness running down his throat like honey, and when it reached his stomach, he felt a glow of contentment. He smiled at the sheer joy of it.

'There, I told you,' said Geoffrey, 'you've been touched.'

'Stuff your nonsense. That was the best thing I've eaten in my life.'

'No good will come of it.'

'We'll see.'

They went home. Matthew saved the cake for as long as he could, just taking small crumbs at a time, but eventually it was all gone. For a while he was sad, but then he realised that he could bring the memory of the taste to his mouth; and when he did that, the same glow came to his stomach and the same smile of contentment came to his face.

So, when the rain was pelting down and Geoffrey was cursing his lot, Matthew would have a sweet smile on his face. People began to wonder if perhaps Matthew had been turned a bit simple, because Geoffrey had told them about the peel and the cake. But they soon revised this opinion. Matthew had become a man who could spot his luck. He caught the eye of the lord of the manor, who seeing that he was a trustworthy sort, entrusted him with various important tasks such as delivering messages or making sure the harvest was gathered in properly. These going well, he appointed Matthew the village reeve, so that he had to sort out all the small disputes and ill-feeling that a small community is prone to. This he did with such good grace that he caught the eye of the village beauty, the one all the other men fancied but were too tongue-tied to talk to sensibly. They married and had some fine children, and were able to set up a farm of their own. Matthew's stock always seemed to do well at market and his crops kept free of diseases, so he and his family prospered. Some people might have taken against him because of his good luck but he was such a happy and good-natured fellow that few begrudged him his happiness.

Matthew never heard the fairies again, nor tasted a fairy cake but the memory made him a contented man for the rest of his days. Geoffrey, strangely, remained a ploughman all his life.

Now, it must be said that the fairies of Inkberrow are not as well-disposed as other fairies in the county, and that is all the fault of the Church. Sometime in the nineteenth century, it was decided that the old church should be torn down and rebuilt on what was considered a more suitable location. Unfortunately, this was a spot where the fairies lived. When work on the new church started, whatever was built in one day was torn down during the night, so that the builders had to start from scratch. This carried on over several weeks, and it looked like the church would never be finished. Those that understood the land said it would be best to put the church back where it was, so as not to upset the fair folk.

At first the vicar thought that this was all superstitious nonsense and that human vandalism was at work; probably associated with the unpopular tithes that he collected as his due. But he was eventually persuaded to splash holy water over the stones. After that, the stones were never moved again and the building work could carry on until the church was finished.

Yet, for many years afterwards, when people happened to be alone in the churchyard, they occasionally reported hearing voices lamenting, 'Neither sleep, neither lie, for Inkberrow's ting-tang hangs so high.'

So incomers who move into the countryside and then complain about the church bells are only following in a long tradition.

TEN

THE LEGEND OF RAGGEDSTONE HILL

In the Middle Ages, it was not a difficult decision to decide what job you would do. A girl would know that, when she grew up, she would be working in the home, either her own or someone else's. Boys would do what their fathers did, so if your father was a knight, you would expect to become one. If he was a peasant, that was what you could expect. The only exception was the clergy. At least before the Great Pestilence struck, there was not enough land for every boy to become a knight or a peasant, so younger sons might find themselves being given to God and spend all their life in the Church. Even here there was class distinction; the son of a lord would expect to make bishop or at least abbot, while the son of a peasant was unlikely to make it beyond monk.

It was not all bad news. The hours might be long but you were guaranteed a roof over your head and regular meals, at least outside Lent and the many other fast days in the calendar. That was more than most people could hope for. There was, however, one major disadvantage; a monk was not allowed to consort with girls. In fact, even to look at one was considered a terrible temptation that should be avoided if at all possible.

Some young men did not mind too much, but not so Brother John. He was a handsome fellow, tall and athletically built. Unfortunately the only inheritance his father could provide for him was just sufficient to allow John to be taken in by the Benedictine monks. This had been well enough when he was a young child, but now that he was entering into manhood, he found himself thinking about life outside the routines of monastic life and the more he thought about them, the more pleasurable the life that he was denied seemed to become.

After his noviciate, John was sent to St Giles Priory at Little Malvern. This was a small place, with only a dozen monks, and where everyone knew each other's business. The Benedictines were great healers, with a wide knowledge of plants and how they could be used for the benefit of Man. As a fit and intelligent youth, it fell to John to go out and gather the herbs the herbalist needed. This was not an arduous task. While some of the older monks were frightened of going outside the walls, John looked forward to it as a delight and providing the possibility of adventure.

One spring morning, Brother John went out to collect some plants that he knew grew by the side of a stream some way from the priory. The day was hot, which made his woollen habit scratchy and uncomfortable. How much would he have given to be allowed to take it off and feel the light wind on his body? The wood was full of bluebells, and in the sun, their fragrance was heavy and almost overpowering. He turned a corner that lead to the stream and then stopped short. Sitting on the bank was a young woman, dangling her feet in the water.

Before he could look away she lifted them out, and he had a good look of her shapely feet and her long, brown legs glistening with water; and above the knee, where the brown gave way

to paler skin until hidden by her smock. Hearing his approach, she turned and smiled at him over her bare shoulder.

Hurriedly Brother John turned away, his face bright red. At a furious pace, he went back to the priory. At first the herbalist was furious that he had not come back with the plants but, when he saw the state he was in, made him sit in the shade until the office of Matins. John could not get the memory of the girl out of his mind, nor the shape of those legs or that smile. The herbalist watched him closely, fearing some serious illness, but although he had a fever, no other symptoms seemed to present themselves, so the herbalist allowed him to resume his duties. John tried to concentrate on the prayers and the singing, but all too often his mind would wander back outside the walls of the priory. But he could not be dissuaded, the following day, from going back out to gather the plants he had not been able to retrieve the day before.

He was very disappointed when he found the river bank deserted. He gathered his plants and walked back to the priory, all the time hoping to catch a glimpse of the girl through the trees; but he had no such luck. So his life returned to normal, although it seemed to John that it was a bit emptier than it had been before.

Then, a few weeks later, he was collecting plants over towards Welland. He was engrossed in the task of looking for the right variety when he was stopped dead in his tracks by the sound of singing. This was not the heavy plainsong that he was used to, but a light, female voice. Although he could not catch all the words, he heard enough to know it was not a religious song she was singing. He followed the sound until he came to a clearing. Peeping from behind a bush, he saw a woman collecting plants, just as he had been doing. He moved closer to get a better view, but stepped on a dry twig that cracked like a clap of thunder.

The woman stood up and looked in John's direction. 'Come out and let me see what you are!'

John wanted to run but he found himself walking out into the clearing. She looked him up and down and John blushed furiously.

'Are you after my secrets, monk?'

'What do you mean?' said John, aghast.

'Wanting to see what plants I am picking, so you can go and tell.'
No, I was just …'

'… Looking. Yes, I can see that.'

If John had blushed before, he went an even deeper red now, but the woman just laughed and beckoned him over. He could do nothing but obey, although he knew that talking to a woman would mean he would have to do penance when he confessed his fault. She started showing what plants she had collected and what their uses were, but all he could think of was the proximity of this woman.

Eventually she saw that he was taking no notice. 'And what ails you, young monk?' she asked, already knowing the answer. She took a long, hard look at him and then leant forward and kissed him on the lips. John's world exploded in the sensation. She took his hand and led him back to her cottage where she showed him that the body was a thing of joy rather than something that always needed curbing.

From then on he was assiduous in his herb collecting, taking every opportunity that presented itself to go outside the priory walls. He found a way of climbing over the walls in the darkness of night, although he made sure to be back in time for Prime, the morning office, which took place before dawn. But, it being a small place, he could not avoid suspicion. Once he was helping the herbalist put together a poultice for a brother who had cut himself badly while digging. 'Aren't you going to add feverfew, for the fever?' asked John innocently.

'Who told you that?' said the herbalist indignantly. 'The body must fight the devil by itself. Anyone who tells you anything else is a fool, or worse.'

Brother John muttered his apologies but, after that, the herbalist kept an eye on him. Brother John was in love, not just with his lady but with the whole world, which now seemed a wonderful place. As we all know, it is difficult to leave those we love. One summer's morning he woke up in his lover's arms to the sound of birdsong. It was warm and light, and for a moment he was happy. Then a terrible realisation struck him. He was late for Prime.

Quickly he dressed, kissed the woman goodbye and ran to the priory. His heart sank as he saw that the great door was already open. As soon as he entered he was taken aback to see the Prior, who interrogated him in the chapel.

Now the Prior was a bitter man who thought he could have done a lot better than this small priory in the middle of nowhere. He often made the other monks suffer for it, and he was certainly going to make John suffer for it now. It did not take long for him to extract the truth from the young man, who could not bring himself to lie in these sacred surroundings. But he would not tell the Prior the name of the woman because he feared what that might mean for her.

'Very well,' said the Prior. 'You have behaved like a beast, and you will be treated like a beast. Every day you will crawl on all fours, from the foot of Raggedstone Hill to its summit, and there say prayers for your forgiveness; you will do this until you tell me the name of the woman you have sinned with.'

So John was taken to the hill and obediently started to climb. Not only did he have the brambles, nettles and gorse, but also small sharp blocks of stone that give the hill its name. By the time he reached the top he was bruised and bleeding, but he sincerely prayed for forgiveness, for the enormity of what he had done had hit him. He was forced to repeat the agony on his way down.

For many days this went on. The cuts, despite everything that the herbalist tried, became infected and his bruises never had time to heal. His brother monks went to the Prior and begged him to end the penance but the Prior was implacable. Until John named the woman who had led him into sin, the ordeal would continue.

At last, one day when Brother John was struggling to the top, barely conscious in the fever that held him, he saw a strange sight. A long shadow resembling a cloud emerged from between the twin peaks of the hill, throwing its darkness down the hill to the monks standing below. A desperate new strength filled him and he got uneasily to his feet.

'No prayers today,' he cried. 'Instead, I put a curse on my punishers. May any whom this shadow falls upon die before their time, as I do.'

With that, he threw himself off the peak into the valley below. The other monks were terrified and ran back to the priory to pray, despite the Prior lashing them with his tongue for being so superstitious. Within a month he was dead of a wasting disease, and whatever the priory had been before, it now became a sad, demoralised place. In 1480 Bishop Alcock found the place a great ruin, and sent the monks and Prior to Gloucester Abbey for two years 'by reason of their demerits'.

Meteorologists now tell us that there is indeed a strange phenomenon associated with the place; not a shadow caused by the sun but a shrouding mist that appears at times, creating the appearance of a shadow. And those who fall into its shade do seem to suffer ill fate. Among the most notable victims have been the Duke of Clarence, shortly before he was arrested and drowned in a cask of wine; Richard III, the last English king to be killed in battle; and his nephew, Edward V, one of the princes in the Tower and Cardinal Wolsey, shortly before he fell from power.

So, if you go walking in the southern Malverns, take care, and make sure you do not fall under the shadow of Raggedstone Hill.

A HORSE
CALLED DRAGON

Until very recently, historians took little interest in oral history. They preferred history that was written down, not only because the source was more easily checked, but also they believed it was more reliable. We have all played the game 'Chinese whispers', where even simple messages can be completely garbled in several tellings, as in the hopefully apocryphal military command, 'send up reserves, we're going to advance,' which turned into, 'send two and six, we're going to a dance.'

That position is gradually changing, as it is being found that folk memories can, in fact, be remarkably accurate and long-lasting. For centuries the Battle of Bosworth was thought to have taken place at one particular place which fitted the landscape described in contemporary chronicles. All the books and all the maps and tourist signs followed accordingly, despite local people always insisting that it was fought some several miles away from that point. Then detectorists discovered the detritus of battle, armour, arrowheads, even cannon balls, exactly where the local people said they would be. The history books had to be rewritten. The following story is an indication of just how long folk memory can last.

Some time ago a young folklorist was going about the byways of Worcestershire doing research for a book he hoped to write about folklore in the area. Very sensibly, he was spending much of his time in local pubs, because he found it was relatively easy to get talking to strangers in such places, and people were more prepared to tell him stories.

He found himself at the Chequers at Cutnall Green. It was a warm day, so he was able to sit outside with his pint, where he found an old man who must have been very old indeed, because he was wearing a smock when that item of clothing had long since fallen out of fashion. In a short while they were joined by a carter who had with him a fine black horse.

They were not long into their conversation when the horse became restless and started making clear indications that he wanted to go, seeing no reason why their stay should be prolonged.

'Easy Dragon, easy boy!' said the carter, in that quiet way that horsemen have when dealing with their four-legged colleagues.

'Tell me,' said the folklorist, 'I've noticed that black horses are often called Dragon in these parts. Is there any reason why that should be so?'

'You're right there,' the carter replied, 'but the reason for it, I don't know.'

The folklorist's heart fell. He had been hoping to be able to complete a few hundred words on the point.

'All I can say,' the carter continued, 'is that black horses have been called Dragon in our family as long ago as when the French came.'

'When on earth was that?' asked the surprised folklorist, who thought he knew his history and was not aware the French had ever invaded Worcestershire.

'Can't rightly say,' said the carter. 'I think it might have been in my grandfather's time or possibly a bit before. We were farmers over Martley way then. Anyway, this is the story my father told me and his father told him. The French came and they were causing all kind of trouble. My ancestor decided that he and his family better get out of it, but he left it a bit late because the Frenchies were already coming over the hill by the time he was ready to leave, you know what farmers are like; always fussing about.

'Anyway, all he had time to do was saddle up his fine black horse that was called Dragon, with his little lad up in front of him and his wife behind him and gallop off as fast as the poor old horse could go with this weight on him. The Frenchies started firing at them, but the good old horse kept going and got away from them, and there was nothing those Frenchies could do about it.

'Eventually he came to Worcester Bridge, where he had to stop. As soon as the horse was still, the poor old woman fell off and they found that she was dead; she had been killed by the French. She had been shot but stayed on the horse until it got to Worcester, and that's a true tale.'

The folklorist paid for the story in the currency of the pub, a pint of best bitter. He chatted away for some time, and then went back to his lodgings and wrote up the story in his notebook. He was happy enough with his afternoon's work. It was a quaint story that showed how fantastical folk tales could get. Then he forgot all about it until a few months later, when he was talking to a historian friend of his who had an interest in horse racing. The man was going on a bit about a particular hope that he had concerning a runner in a forthcoming race and mentioned that it was a black horse. This reminded the folklorist about the horse called Dragon and he told it to his friend the story as a way of changing the subject.

He was in the middle of a very enjoyable moan about the shocking lack of knowledge about history among the common people when he noticed that his friend was looking strangely solemn.

'Actually,' said the historian, 'in a way the French did come to Worcestershire. In the Owain Glyndŵr rebellion at the beginning of the fifteenth century, there was a large French contingent in the Welsh force that invaded England and got as far as Worcestershire. In fact they did come as far as Martley and made their headquarters on Woodbury Hill. If you think of the poor woman being shot by an arrow rather than a bullet, there's nothing in that tale that could not have happened. And there's something else convincing about it. You say the farmer stopped on Worcester Bridge. Well, why would you? With the

French after you, surely you would ride fast over it. But, at that time, there was a gatetower in the middle of the bridge where everyone would be stopped and checked.'

The folklorist was nonplussed. Could that story have been passed down through the generations of one family for over 500 years? He resolved to treat oral stories with a bit more respect in the future, and was no doubt a better folklorist because of it.

Roy Palmer, in his magnificent work, *The Folklore of Hereford and Worcester*, comments that horsemen in the area seemed to choose their horses' names from a select, traditional list, the most popular being: Bert, Blackbird, Bonny, Bounce, Bowler, Boxer, Brandy, Captain, Charlie, Darby, Diamond, Dobbin, Dragon, Duke, Flower, Gilbert, Jerry, Jolly, Lion, Lively, Short, Smiler, Snip, Spanker, Surly and Tommy.

Did this show a certain lack of imagination in these men? I think it more likely that the names carried their own power that each horse of that name inherited and then passed on to the next. We all know that naming a child is an important thing. How much more so the naming of a companion with whom you might share more hours than you do with your wife?

TWELVE

THE BALLAD
OF SIR RYALAS

Sir Humphrey Stafford of Grafton had a reputation to keep up. These were difficult times, with a weak, almost idiotic, king on the throne. No man, not even one of the mighty Staffords, could be sure that his lands and his riches would remain his.

One day he went hunting. To ease the weight on his mind he liked nothing more than to go out and kill things, perhaps a boar or a deer, maybe even a wolf; there were still some said to be lurking in nearby Feckenham Forest.

Somehow he became separated from his companions. As dusk approached they had all returned to the castle, but still there was no sign of Sir Humphrey. They became concerned, because the forest at night was a dangerous place, and if anything had happened to Sir Humphrey they were likely to lose their employment.

Finally, as the last red rays of the setting sun were disappearing behind the hill, they saw a rider approaching. They recognised their lord from the way he rode. As he came closer, their relief turned to joy because they saw he had a dead boar across his saddle. There would be plenty of food to eat tonight, and Sir Humphrey would be in a good mood.

The knight rode into the courtyard and threw the boar down in triumph. Then he saw the look on his men's faces. In truth it was not a large boar. In fact it could be easily mistaken for a domestic pig. Irritably he jumped down from the horse.

'You wouldn't believe the trouble I've had to get that,' he said. 'And, if you fetch me a jug of wine, I will tell you all about it.'

The jug was duly fetched and, after Sir Humphrey had quenched his thirst, he began his tale.

'I don't know where you got to, but I followed a brook until I had penetrated right into the heart of the forest. By noon I had come to a place that I did not recognise and was on the point of turning back when I heard a cry. Looking up I saw

a young maiden sitting in the topmost branches of a great oak. It struck me that, wearing the dress that she was, it was not the most lady-like of positions. "What are you doing up there?" I called, and I did not hear all of her response, but it seemed that the young lady had climbed up there to escape a terrifying wild boar that was terrorizing the neighbourhood.'

'"Where is the boar now?" I asked her, and again, I did not catch all her response but I took for her meaning that if I blew my horn it would probably appear. Naturally that is what I did, and almost immediately, there was a great rustling in the bushes and this great boar burst out of it.

'Now it might not be so much to look at now but, with its hackles raised and rage and bloodlust in its eyes, it was terrible enough. I got down off my horse and drew my sword just before the beast charged and then we fought, gentlemen. We fought for what must have been four hours or more, neither of us gaining the upper hand and neither of us willing to give way. At last, as the day was turning to dusk, I started to gain the advantage. I saw the look of defeat come into the creature's eyes and it started to look around for a way of escape.

'But I was too fast for it. As it turned I gave it a mighty thrust with my sword, gutting it from its head to its toes, the very wound you see on it now gentlemen.'

After this recital his followers standing around began to applaud and congratulate him for his prowess. But, just at that moment there was a commotion at the gates and an old woman, swearing profusely, pushed her way past the guards and approached the group.

'You!' she cried out, pointing at Sir Humphrey. 'Hey, you! You've killed my spotted pig. What am I to do for food this winter now?'

Without thinking, Sir Humphrey drew his sword and cut her head off. The old woman and the head fell down next to the pig. A gasp of horror escaped from the men. Even in these lawless times, no one, not even a lord, could go around cutting old lady's heads off with impunity.

'It's all right gentlemen,' said Sir Humphrey. 'That was the wild woman of the woods, in league with the boar. If we had let her live she would have bewitched us.'

Now everyone really knew that it was old Nancy Bridges who lived in a hovel on the outskirts of the forest but, with Sir Humphrey with a sword in his hand, no one was tempted to say anything or to say, 'Yes, but what happened to the lady up the tree?'

So the story of mighty Sir Humphrey and his terrible fight with the boar became the one that was spread around. Eventually some wit took the tune of a north country ballad of Sir Ryalas and adapted Sir Humphrey's story to it. It became a popular song around Worcestershire. Like all good songs it had a chorus: 'Well wind the horn, good hunter … As thou art a jovial hunter.' Those who knew the dour Sir Humphrey thought it was very funny singing that.

Eventually the ballad even reached the court in London. Now, at that time, the king had to show that he was the biggest bastard in a court of bastards, but King Henry, although he was the son of the warlike Henry V, much preferred skipping about and smelling flowers rather than telling all those shouty men to behave. Naturally they took the hint and started behaving just as they pleased.

One of these shouty men, the Duke of Suffolk, had got himself murdered in Kent. It tends to happen when you throw your weight around. The courtiers told the king that dukes could not be murdered just like that, otherwise where would it end? They persuaded him that the people of Kent must be punished for allowing the Duke to get himself murdered. The people of Kent thought differently, not liking their homes being burned for something that was not of their making and now an angry mob, led by Jack Cade, was on its way to London to sort the matter out.

The king remembered the story about Sir Ryalas and sent for Sir Humphrey Stafford to sort out Jack Cade as he had sorted out the mighty boar. Sir Humphrey was overjoyed – there was probably a dukedom or something in it for him – so he set out with his men, wearing his best armour, with his gold flag with a red chevron proudly flying in front of him.

The mob had reached Blackheath, which was then open countryside, when Sir Humphrey caught up with it. It was a big mob, but Sir Humphrey's men were better armed, swords against pitchforks, so Sir Humphrey knew he could not lose. He ordered a charge, and sure enough, the peasants turned and ran. Sir Humphrey's heart almost burst with excitement. Now there would be some fine killing and then he would be rich. Then he heard shouts from behind him. Turning his head he saw that his men were being attacked by a group of peasants that had hidden behind some gorse bushes. And now those ahead had turned and were coming back towards him, and they had been joined by even more – it was an ambush!

Sir Humphrey might have been a fool but he was no coward. He continued the charge right into the centre of the mob, hacking and hewing until he was dragged from his horse, stabbed with a pitchfork and had his throat slit. His fine armour was stripped off him and given to Jack Cade, who wore it until he made the mistake of believing an offer of free pardon and was himself hunted down and killed.

What was left of Sir Humphrey was taken back to Worcestershire and buried in the parish church of Bromsgrove. After his wife died, some thirty years later, a fine marble tomb was built for them both, complete with his crest of a boar's head. In later generations, to complete the story, it was suggested that she was the lady up the tree and a final verse was added to the ballad of Sir Ryalas.

In Bromsgrove church they both do lie,
Well wind the horn good hunter!
There the wild boar is pictured by
Sir Ryalas, the jovial hunter.

THIRTEEN

THE OLD WOMAN OF ODDINGLEY

Back in what we like to call the Middle Ages, the people of the village of Oddingley would not see a doctor from one year to the next. Doctors were only for the rich, who could pay for them. In some ways this was actually quite a good thing, because medicine in those days relied on a very hazy knowledge of the human body, and remedies that were based on what had been done before rather than any experience of them actually doing any good.

Therefore rural areas tended to rely on a local wise woman, someone with a knowledge of herbs and an effective bedside manner so that, at the very least, the placebo effect would have a chance of coming into play.

At this time the village of Oddingley was blest with a particularly fine wise woman. She had grown old in service to her community and had built up a great fund of knowledge in the way that the world worked. The people of Oddingley respected her and gave what they could in payment, although this was not very much, so she lived in what was little more than a hovel with only a couple of cats for company. She was the sort of person who would always try to do good to both man and beast, but she was also someone you did not want to get on the wrong side of.

One day she was out gathering herbs when she heard the sound of horses trotting along the road. This was not a totally pleasing sound because the meeting between the rich and the poor could go one of several ways, not all of them good. So she stepped off the road and waited for the horsemen to go by.

There were four of them. Their horses were big and well cared for and their clothes, though covered in dust from travel, were obviously expensive. They were young and looked as if they had no cares in the world, and her heart fell as the horses slowed as they came abreast of her.

The youth at their head was a giant of a man; she had never seen one so big and strong. She could see that he would turn the heads of many a woman, but she could also see that he knew it. However he touched his hat to her in a very gallant fashion and said politely, 'Good morning to you, mother.'

'Good morning, young sirs.'

Another of the party, so slim and pretty looking that the old woman could have mistaken him for a maid, sneered, 'So old woman, tell us, when was it that you were last kissed because of your beauty?'

'Long enough for my liking,' said the old woman. 'Though I confess I have never been kissed by four brothers before.'

There was a gasp from the riders and the pretty one crossed himself for protection. 'She's a witch!' he cried to the others, the colour draining from his fair cheeks.

'There is no witchery here, nor any trickery neither,' she replied. 'It's as plain as your faces that you are related. 'Though you look quite different, you all have your mother's eyes and your father's nose. The village simpleton could see that you were brothers.'

Then the one who had been last in the procession urged his horse forward. He was smaller than the others, sat more crooked in the saddle and had an anxious frown on his face, while the others looked as if no trouble could torment them. He gave her a low bow, mocking in its condescension. 'If you were a witch, you could tell us our fortunes and then we would give you a fine gold coin for your trouble.'

'Young gentlemen,' says the old woman, 'knowing your fortunes is a thing best left alone. They are bad enough when they come, without worrying about 'em aforehand.'

'Then just tell us the good bits,' said the second brother. 'Leave out the bad bits, and you would just be wishing us well.'

'My lad,' she said, 'I'll wish you all as well as I can but my wishes won't mend what's got to be.'

But they kept on worrying at her and she did not want to annoy such rich and powerful young men, and in truth, the gold coin would come in pretty useful when the winter came along, so she gave in and agreed to tell their fortunes. She turned to the eldest, the one who had spoken to her first.

'Sir, what fortune would you like to have?'

'Easy for me, that one. I'd like to be a great king and a great conqueror, and defeat all my enemies.'

'And how would you want to die?'

'I'd like to die like a great king, in my castle, with my people mourning me and leaving my crown to my heirs forever.'

'Well wished it is. And what do you wish for?' she said, turning to the second brother.

'I don't want all the trouble of being king, but I want to be a brave knight and die in battle at the moment of victory.'

'Well wished it is. And what do you wish for, my pretty gentleman?'

'No kings or battles for me,' the third young man laughed. 'Fine clothes and fine horses and plenty of wine and dancing, that's for me. The love of many young ladies and soft beds to lie on is what I want.'

'And how would you die?'

'I don't want to die at all, but if I must, I want to drown in wine.'

'Well wished it is.' Finally she turned to the youngest. 'And what do you want, young man with the haunting smile?'

'I may not be as tall and straight as my brothers, but I'd like to be a great fighter and ride down my enemies so all the great knights of the land will want to follow me. Fame is what I want and, when I die, let it be in battle, leaving a name that will sound down the ages.'

'Well wished it is. So, my lads, I will promise you all the best parts of your wishes. You will have what you asked for, but perhaps not quite as you expect it.'

'How so?'

'I reckon it's the way of the world, my dears. We all wants a lot, and if we're lucky, we gets a bit of what we wants, but there's always something a-missing and when we get what we wants, it's never the same as we reckoned it would be. Howsoever, I wish you all as well as I can and God bless you all.'

The eldest dug into his purse and tossed the old woman a gold coin as had been promised and they rode off, laughing at each other's fortunes as only the young can.

The old woman walked home, grateful for the gold coin, but shaking her head at the fate that awaited these fine young men. For these were the four Mortimer brothers, sons of the powerful Duke of York who would shortly lead the Yorkist side in what later became known as the Wars of the Roses.

The eldest of them was Edward, Earl of March, who would indeed get his wish to become king, going down in history as Edward IV. He was greatly mourned by his people because he died young, leaving his eldest son but a child, and reopening the deep wounds caused by the civil war. As to his heirs being kings forever, well, all royalty is so closely related that our present queen can claim descent from Edward. But his son was one of the Princes in the Tower, who disappeared into that fearsome place within a few months of becoming king and was never seen again.

The second was Edmund, Earl of Rutland. He got his wish to be a warrior. His father took the boy with him to fight at the Battle of Wakefield. But the battle was lost and his chaplain persuaded Edmund to flee. It was already too late, and they were captured by Lord Clifford's men. At first Lord Clifford did not recognise him, but then the chaplain blurted out who it was, thinking that Edmund's importance would ensure his safety.

'Your father killed my father,' said Clifford, 'so now I take my revenge.' Forcing Edmund to kneel, Clifford took his great sword and sliced the boy's head clean off. He was just seventeen. In a sense he did die at the moment of victory, but it was the victory of his enemies. His head and that of his father were taken to York and stuck on poles above the city gates, with paper crowns upon them.

The third, the pretty one, was George, Duke of Clarence. He did indeed live a life of pleasure, but his position meant that he could not keep out of politics completely. Increasingly resentful and jealous of his surviving brothers, he conspired against them but the treason was discovered. He was arrested and confined in the Tower of London where he was 'privately executed'. Tradition has it that he was drowned in a butt of malmsey wine, in tribute to his heavy drinking; a method devised by his younger brother.

This, the last, the anxious and haunted one, was Richard, Duke of Gloucester. He did indeed become a noted commander, skilful in tactics so that men were pleased to follow him. After his brother Edward's death, he feared for his own life at the hands of Edward's widow's family and seized the throne himself. Despite what Shakespeare says he seems to have been a good king, introducing the Court of Requests, a form of legal aid, and the first bail system.

After Henry Tudor's invasion, Richard confronted him at the Battle of Bosworth. Seeing the battle was lost, Richard made one last, brave charge, hoping to kill Henry. In this he almost succeeded but was cut down just before he could reach him. Perhaps, for a second, he thought it was the moment of victory. But history is written by the winners. Instead of honour, his name is synonymous with tyranny and evil, the archetypal wicked uncle.

So, remember the words of the old lady of Oddingley. Sometimes it is better not to know what fortune has in store.

FOURTEEN

THE TYTHING WITCHES

Now some of you might know Worcester quite well and have been past the place they call the Tything a few times. Perhaps you have found it a bit spooky and feel a little uneasy when you go there? If that is the case you are right to do so, because a long time ago, the place was the home of two witches. It was said of them that if there was something that they did not know about the black arts, it was because the devil was keeping it for himself. This was somewhat unfair, because the two old ladies sold charms and spells to ease the lot of the poorer class of townsfolk who could afford nothing better. They had spells to cure warts, potions for the toothache and charms to find that which was lost. I cannot vouch for the effectiveness of their wares but I do know that they made but a poor living, although that was most likely down to the poverty of the people around them more than their lack of skill. In fact, they would have been hard pushed to keep body and soul together if it was not for the carts.

These were the days before tarmacking or any other form of paving for city roads. The carts coming in and out of Worcester just rolled over the earth, and inevitably, churned up the

ground something terrible, especially in wet weather. The carters noticed that their wagons had a particular knack of getting
stuck right outside the old ladies' house.

If this happened, then one or other of the old women would
come out of their house and enquire if the carter had any small
coins about them that, out of charity, they could afford to pass
into the hand of a poor old widow woman who never did anyone
any harm. If the coins were forthcoming she would wave her
hands over the cart and say, 'God bless the cart!', upon which the
horses would set off again, as easily as if the cart had no load on
it. The carters talked amongst themselves about it, but none of
them had the nerve to say anything to the old women or refuse
to hand over the money. It did not happen every time, and the
toll was not as excessive as some of the great lords charged, so the
carters thought it best to let them get on with it.

One day a salt cart came bouncing along the road and, as
luck would have it, there was a new man on board who had not
made the trip before. Sure enough the cart stuck fast just before
the old ladies' house, which greatly surprised the carter because
it had not rained in days, and the ground was as hard as stone.

After a short time one of the women came out of her house
and made her usual enquiry.

'Don't trouble me now, mother. I have to see what's wrong
with this damned cart.'

He got down and went to take a look at the horses. He was
surprised to see a long straw lying across the wheel-horse's back,
but he took out his knife and cut it in two. The old woman
screamed and the horses bolted, and the carter had to run after
them, so he did not see what he left behind. There on the road
was the other old woman, cut clean in two, and a great pool of
blood oozing into the earth.

That was the end of carts getting stuck at the Tything; the old woman that was left not seeming too keen on collecting the toll anymore. However this meant that the old woman became very poor. Her neighbours took pity on her and paid what they could for her charms and potions, but it was still a hard struggle for her to keep body and soul together.

One day she had managed to collect enough to buy a loaf of bread, so she went into Worcester to the baker that she favoured. She was coming back out of town after making her purchase, the bread warm in her hands, when she saw a troop of armed men riding towards her. As if overawed by their armour glinting in the sun and their shiny spears, she remained rooted to the spot in the middle of the road as they galloped towards her.

'Get out of my way!' shouted their leader, forced to bring his horse to a stop. 'We have important business in the city.'

'Yes, your lordship,' says the old woman, bobbing very respectful-like and proceeding to do so, if a little slowly, on account of her age.

The leader, a young man wearing a fine silk doublet, whose cloak alone cost more than all the money she had seen in her life, decided to use the time to amuse his men.

'Tell me old woman, where did you get that loaf of bread?'

'In Worcester, it please you sir,' answered the woman, giving him a nod that might be interpreted as a curtsy.

'And how much did you pay for it?'

'A penny, captain.'

'Well, when I've finished with this town, you won't be able to get a loaf of bread for a penny or sixpence or for any amount of money. I'm here to collect the king's taxes, and I'm going to find every last farthing or there will be trouble.'

All his men laughed, but the old woman pursed her lips, which the young man did not find a very pretty sight.

'That you won't,' she said. 'You'll never get to the town, and you'll never be done with it, neither.'

This caused even more hilarity in the ranks.

'Never get to town, you old fool?' said the lord, sounding very bitter. 'Why, we're nearly there already. Look, there's the gate just over there, or can't your old eyes see it?' By now some of his men were almost falling off their horses, they were laughing so much at their leader's wit.

'Oh you'll get to the gate all right, but no further. Stones you are, all the lot of you, and stones you will remain until Judgement Day.' With that she pointed her finger at them in a very peculiar way. Then she hobbled off in the direction of her home.

Impatiently, the young lord spurred his horse forward. As soon as his horse came to the gate the creature collapsed, taking the young man with it, and all the other horses did exactly the same. When the dust cleared, all the people of Worcester saw was a heap of grey stones lying by the roadside.

Now the city fathers were in a quandary. They did not want a heap of stones right up against their gate, but neither did they want these soldiers collecting taxes, especially given that if they were restored to normality, they were not likely to be in the best of moods, given their adventures. The old woman let it be known that she had laid a word on them, and that they should stay as stones until someone came by the light of a new moon and put a loaf of bread on each stone and said the Lord's Prayer over it. Nobody fancied the idea, in case it annoyed the old woman, and so the stones stayed where they were.

A short while after the old lady died, but still the stones remained by the side of the road. Even after her death, people did not like the idea of crossing her. But, over time, this fear decreased. Eventually one young man from Worcester decided to have a go. Opinion was divided as to him being extremely brave or just a bit gallous, mischievous. Whichever way it was, he said he was going to do it for the sake of the poor soldiers, though if it made him famous and anyone was to give him a few coins for his trouble, that would not go amiss.

The young man waited until the next new moon; then he went to one of the bakers in the town and told him of the wonderful opportunity that awaited him if the baker was to give him a large quantity of loaves. His name would go down in the history of the city as the baker who provided the bread that freed the unfortunate soldiers.

As luck would have it, the baker did have some stale loaves that he had not been able to sell that day, and was happy to let the young man have them. So, carrying his basket, the young man set off for the Tythings. He put a loaf on every stone and then said the Lord's Prayer over it. Eventually he came to the last but one stone. He put a loaf on top of it and then he started reciting the prayer.

He had just got to the part, 'Forgive us our trespasses,' when the stone turned into a live horse and reared up above him, its hooves glinting in the moonlight. He was so scared that he dropped his basket and ran for his life.

So the stones remained stones, as they do to this very day. No one dared ever go through this procedure ever again and, as far as I know, they are there yet.

FIFTEEN

THE LONELY OGRE

Once there was an ogre. The ogre lived on top of the Malvern Hills, and made his living by eating any travellers that were misguided enough to try to travel along that path.

In those days it was a desolate and rocky place, but from there the ogre could see the beautiful farmland of Worcestershire stretched out beneath him. He could see the people of Malvern having parties, falling in love and bringing up their families. The ogre was very lonely on his hilltop since his wife had left him (ogres are not terribly good at relationships), and he wondered what he could do about it.

One day, he was lucky enough to eat a magician. With the magician's skill inside him, he knew that if he took a very deep breath he could draw up all the warmth and contentment from down in Malvern and breathe it into himself. So that is what he did. One morning when he could see the people going about their tasks, he took a deep breath and sucked in all the warmth and contentment that was out there in the shire.

Now the people of Malvern noticed the change immediately. Masters fell out with servants, wives fell out with husbands and the children just could not get along with anybody.

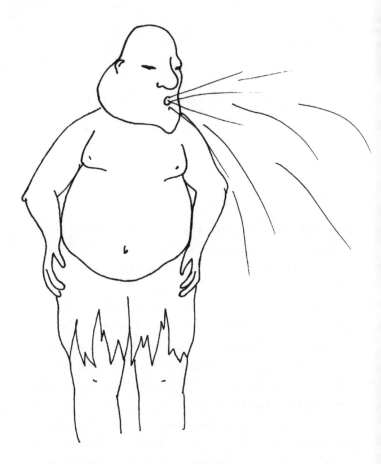

Desperate to stop all the fights that were breaking out and the language in the street that was absolutely appalling, the lord of the manor, John Hornyold, called in a cunning man to find out what the problem was.

The cunning man saw at once where the trouble lay: 'It's the ogre who lives up on the Hills. He has sucked in all the warmth and contentment from your lives.'

Now the people knew what to do.

'Let's get all our strong young men, and they can go up and kill the ogre.' Because now they had no warmth and contentment in their lives they could only think of solving their problems through violence.

'No!' said the cunning man. 'That won't do. If you kill the ogre, all the warmth and contentment will die with him and you will be no better off than you are now.'

So the people all stood around, not knowing what to do but blame each other.

Then Marjorie, John Hornyold's young daughter, stepped forward. She had been tucked up in bed asleep when the ogre had taken his deep breath, so she still had all her warmth and contentment deep in her heart.

'Let me go and talk to the ogre and see what can be done.'

Now the people, having lost all their warmth and contentment, thought it was a reasonable thing to send a young girl to talk to an ogre. Even her father could not see anything against it. So she packed some honey sandwiches and water from the Holy Well and set off to meet the ogre.

Meanwhile, the ogre was not happy. Now that he had warmth and contentment in his heart, he could not bring himself to eat the travellers that went by his cave, so he was starving. When he saw young Marjorie coming up the hill towards him, he knew he must eat something soon or he would die. Yet still he could not bring himself just to jump out and eat her. He felt it would only be polite to engage her in conversation first.

As she came up to his cave, he sauntered out and said, 'You've got a nerve coming up here. Aren't you frightened I'm going to eat you?'

'Possibly,' said the girl. 'But I think someone who has as much warmth and contentment in their heart as you do would think of something better to do with their time.'

'But I'm starving!' cried the ogre. 'If I don't eat someone soon I will die.'

'Best not be hasty,' said the girl. 'Let's sit down here, and you can share my lunch and we can see what can be done.'

So the ogre ate a honey sandwich and he found it was much sweeter than the flesh he was used to, and he drank some water and found it was much better for his thirst than blood. It struck him that this was the first time anyone had ever given him anything, and great tears of sadness ran down his face.

'It seems to me,' said the girl, 'that it is no good having all the warmth and contentment in the world if you are living up here on your own. You only really know what it's like if you share it with other people. Why don't you come back with me and we can all see if we can get along together?'

'No one will want to be friends with me,' cried the ogre.

'Now you're just feeling sorry for yourself,' said the girl. 'It strikes me that you have very little choice in the matter, because you are not going to make much of a living up here in your current state.'

So it was agreed that the ogre would come down with her. When the people saw the ogre approaching, they were terrified and starting running about all over the place, but the girl called them back and explained what was happening. It was agreed that there would be a big party that evening to welcome the ogre.

At first the party was very stiff and formal, with everyone on their best behaviour. But then the ogre started to feel how good it was to be surrounded by people, and he let out a great sigh

of contentment. When he had done that, everyone else found that they were enjoying themselves as well and people started singing and telling jokes, something they had not done for a very long time. The following morning they all agreed that it was the best party they had ever been to.

So the ogre stayed in Malvern, and there was not a party or celebration that was complete without the ogre somewhere in a corner laughing and joking.

Malvern got a reputation for good fellowship and kindness. A few years later, Queen Elizabeth got to hear about it, and she was so impressed that she granted John Hornyold some land around the Holy Well at South Malvern, on condition that any pilgrim or traveller should be able to rest there and draw refreshment freely from the well; a covenant that is still in place to this day.

Sixteen

The Gentleman Robber

We like to think the gentry lead a life of unsullied pleasure, what with their manor houses and money. Too rich to have to worry about where their next meal was coming from, but not so rich that they had to be plotting and scheming all the time to make more. Sadly that seems not often to be the case; they are prey to all the troubles and sadnesses of this world, just like the rest of us.

Certainly that was true for Edmund Colles, who owned Leigh Court at the time of Elizabeth I. This was a bad time for everyone, with poor harvests and a recession in trade. Edmund must have felt himself one of the 'squeezed middle', with his tenants complaining that they could not pay their rent, and the state expecting higher taxes. He knew that his position was becoming precarious. His outgoings were greater than his incomings, and his savings were dwindling to nothing. He did what he could for a man of his position in society; he sold off a few farms and entered into secret negotiation with Walter Devereux, the MP for Worcester, to sell him Leigh Court and the estate that went with it. But Devereux was a hard bargainer, and Edmund realised that if he did not do something drastic, he would be forced into destitution.

Outwardly he had to appear that nothing was troubling him, because if any hints of his true position got out, he would lose all credit, both financial and social, and he would be lost. So he kept up what show of affluence and generosity he could while constantly being driven almost to distraction by the worry eating away at his soul.

So he was at a tavern in Worcester, drinking with some of his friends and thereby hoping to forget his worries, when he heard the news that would change his life. One of these friends, his tongue loosened by the quantity of wine Edmund had treated him to, mentioned that, later that night, he had to carry a large sum of money back to his home at Cradley.

'Be careful you don't meet with any robbers,' said Edmund, and the moment he said it, he realised that he had a chance of saving his fortune. For the rest of that evening only part of him was present, laughing and drinking with his friends. A good part of him was exultant that he might have found a way of saving himself, and another part was screaming at the danger to which he was opening himself up.

Eventually the party broke up, and Edmund made sure he was one of the first to leave. He saddled his horse and rode out of Worcester. Again, he felt as though his soul was being torn in two. Part of him wanted to ride home and get safely to bed, but the larger part of him, lulled by the drink, was fingering the sword at his hip and thinking how good he would feel if his problems were behind him. Without making the conscious decision he found himself on the road to Cradley. He rode a good way from the town and then started looking for a suitable place to set an ambush.

He came to a bend in the road. The trees here were tall and overhanging. A rider would have to slow down at this point.

It was as perfect a spot as he could be bothered to find in his excited state. He rode past the bend and tied his horse loosely to a tree a little way off the road, but within easy reach. He would need to make a quick escape. He checked that there was nothing distinguishing about his clothing. Fortunately there was no moon, but he took an old cloth out of his saddle bag and tied it across his mouth by way of further disguise. Then, drawing his sword, he went back to the bend and waited.

It seemed an age before he heard the clop, clop of an approaching horse. Peering anxiously through the darkness, he could just see the white blaze on the horse's forehead that marked it out as belonging to his friend. The irritating, self-assured way that the fellow rode also confirmed to Edmund that this was his target.

Edmund waited, hiding in the bushes to the left of the rider, until the horse was level with him. Then he jumped out, grabbed the animal's bridle with one hand, and levelled his sword at the chest of the rider.

'Hold! Give me your saddlebags!' he cried.

But he had not seen that, wary of riding so late at night with so much money, his friend already had his sword firmly in his right hand. Before Edmund knew what was happening, his blade was parried and the sword swooped down on the hand holding the bridle.

Not waiting to see the result of his blow, the rider spurred his horse into a gallop and rode as if he feared all the devils of hell were chasing him. He was greatly relieved when he arrived at his house in Cradley without greater mishap. He called for his groom, who led the sweating horse into the stables. As the shock of the events of the night finally swept over him, the man could do nothing but gabble about his brush with death and his bravery in fighting off an unknown number of bandits. By the light of the candle in the stable, the groom was about to unbridle the horse when he let out a cry of horror and pointed at the horse's head. On the bridle was a severed human hand, still clutching the leather and dripping blood down the horse's neck.

Once he had got over the shock, Colles' friend grimly prised the hand off the bridle. In doing so, he saw that it had a ring on the little finger. Looking more closely he saw it bore the crest of the Colles family. A chill went down his spine. Was not this the hand that had clapped him on the back just hours before? Had it not handed him a bottle of wine as its owner told him to drink up like a good fellow?

Even after the horse was settled, there was no sleep for him that night. He paced his room, planning dire revenge on his one-time friend who had played so false. At the first signs of dawn he assembled as many of his able-bodied men as he could muster and they rode to Leigh Court to demand an explanation. But when they arrived at the court they found the place in uproar, with servants running about like ants that have lost their nest.

Demanding to see Edmund Colles, he was ushered up to the principal bedroom, where he found the man in bed. His face had the pallor of approaching death and the sheets were awash with blood. Edmund clutched the stump of his left arm, which was covered with a sodden bandage that was almost black with the amount of blood on it. All the words that the man had planned went out of his head, as he saw that Edmund Colles would soon be facing a more severe judge than he could ever be.

'I know why you have come,' groaned Edmund, 'and thank God for it. Please, before I die, forgive me for the great sin I have done you.'

'With all my heart,' said the man, all thoughts of retribution removed by pity; then he turned on his heels and left.

Edmund duly died a few hours later and was buried in the family vault in St Edburga's church in Leigh. Yet it seemed his friend's forgiveness was not as effective as might be hoped. For many years afterwards, Edmund Colles' ghost was seen driving a coach pulled by four fire-breathing horses along the road at Leigh, right up over the great tithe barn of the court, and then disappearing into the River Teme. It got so bad that twelve parsons were assembled to lay the ghost. This they did successfully, trapping the spirit in a silver box which they threw into a pool, which was then filled in. Now travellers could walk that road without fear, 'and peaceful ever after slept old Colles' shade' became a well-known local saying, to quiet anyone who became spooked in the night time.

You might think there was something familiar about that story, and that you had heard another like it, of a severed hand found after an attempted crime – something that had happened to a friend of a friend of yours, but set in Hull, or was it Michigan? Shame on him for including an urban legend in a book of folk tales, you will be thinking. In fact, that story was first printed in 1579. Perhaps this is a legend that started in Worcestershire and has now travelled all over the world. Fortunately, for any of us who have to travel the roads of Worcestershire by night, we now know that peaceful ever after sleeps old Colles' shade.

SEVENTEEN

THE MOTHER'S HAND

John Aubrey was an antiquary and gossip in the late seventeenth century, perhaps best known these days for a series of biographical sketches we call 'Brief Lives'. This is one of his stories.

The Pakingtons were a famous Worcestershire family. Sir John Pakington had made a great fortune in the time of Henry VIII. He was a lawyer, and this was a time when if you wanted to become rich and did not mind how you did it, a lawyer was the best thing to be, a bit like being a banker nowadays. King Henry was so impressed with him that he granted John the right to remain seated and to keep his hat on in the king's presence, the only non-member of the royal family to be allowed this privilege. Through his shady dealings he was able to set himself up as lord of the manor at Westwood, north-west of Droitwich.

His grandnephew and heir, another Sir John, was noted for his extravagant way of living. Queen Elizabeth, who was fond of nicknames, called him 'Lusty Pakington'. He had a daughter, whom he married to Sir Walter Long of Draycot, head of another family that had made itself rich by shady legal dealings.

However this lady was not strong, and within a few years of marriage, she died in childbirth, though not before giving birth to a son. This boy, who had been named Thomas, was himself not a robust child and Sir Walter, concerned that he must be sure of an heir, resolved to marry for a second time. He chose a daughter of Sir John Thynne of Longleat, another newly rich family who were more inclined to settle disputes in the courtroom rather than the battlefield.

In the course of time she too gave birth to a son, James, a fine, sturdy creature. So the two boys grew up together, one frail and weak, looking almost as if he were a fairy changeling that the next breeze would knock over; the other a pug-dog of a boy, who was already tormenting flies by the age of two.

The elder child's stepmother, naturally, listened attentively for every cough and sneeze the boy made, hoping that this was a sign that he would soon be at death's door, in which case she would be more than happy to help him through it. But, as so often happens on these occasions, Thomas proved a squeaking gate, which rattles a lot but never completely comes off its hinges. As her husband got older and closer to his death and young Thomas remained on this earth, disinheriting her own son, she decided that she would have to be a little bit more proactive in the matter.

She declared that it was ruining the boy to keep him molly-coddled in the house all the time; he should be out riding. That was the only way that he could be made stronger. Not just that, but he must be sent off hunting, and the huntsman must see to it that he took all the dangerous jumps at speed, and gallop at every opportunity. Unfortunately the dratted child proved to have a good seat and could not be dislodged from the horse, and looked in no likelihood of breaking his neck. Even when he was sent out in the most inclement weather and came back cold and dripping, he seemed to take no harm by it. Indeed, it was seen that the boy did seem to be getting stronger, and Thomas' stepmother was universally celebrated for the good care she had of her stepchild; praise she took through gritted teeth.

Time passed and Sir Walter became more and more frail, and as if he was in some way sucking the strength from his father, Thomas's health prospered. Dame Long was secretly beside herself with worry, though she must make an outward show of happiness that this cuckoo thrived so. When the boy was sixteen, Sir Walter suffered a long illness from which it was for some time feared that he would not recover. That he did was held to be due to his wife's constant care and tenderness. But this scare was sufficient for the lady to steel herself for a more direct attack on the creature that made her life miserable.

For many years she had discussed with James, her own child, the miseries of being a younger son. How he was bound to have to go out in the world to seek his fortune, rather than life the happy life of a gentleman that would be the lot of his brother. He would probably have to become a soldier and go abroad to fight in the bitter Thirty Years War that was then ravaging the continent, with uncertain consequences.

As for Sir Walter, he had once been a hearty, devil-may-care fellow, but his recent illnesses had played on his mind. Like many lawyers, there were deeds in his past that he did not look forward having to explain to his Maker. Increasingly he was being drawn to the Puritan branch of religion, especially that bit that ruled that, the more you indulged yourself in this life, the more sure you were to suffer for it in the next.

One day James sidled up to Thomas just as he was setting off for the stables. They had never been particularly close and Thomas was a little surprised to find James seeking him out.

'What are you up to today?' asked his half-brother.

'Just going for a ride.'

'Come with me then. I'm riding into the village.'

'Father does not like us going there. He says it is a place full of sin.'

'What does the old man know about anything? Don't come if you're frightened.'

'I am not.'

So the two rode to the nearby village. Thomas was surprised about how friendly James was being to him, but having no animosity to the young man, was hopeful that this might be a sign that they could become friends, the way that he thought brothers should.

There were two public attractions in the village, the church and the pub, and James had no attention of heading for the church. Thomas, on the other hand, had never been to the pub before. Of course, he was used to drinking a little beer at mealtimes, but otherwise he was an abstemious lad who was only interested in riding, and was a little bit surprised to find James not only greeted by name but as someone who was likely to bring excitement and good cheer to the morning.

James seemed willing to live up to his reputation, being very generous in treating those who happened to be in the tavern that early in the day. He also let Thomas know that it was a local custom that no one was expected to pay for their drink the first ever time they entered a pub and James would be more than happy to pay for everything. He was also very insistent that they uphold the family honour by matching the yokels drink for drink.

Over time it dawned on Thomas that the room that he was in had become much more crowded than it had been. It was also much warmer. His head seemed to have become much more clouded and it was thus more difficult for him to hold onto his thoughts than he was normally accustomed. It was disconcerting but not altogether unpleasant. Soon he was rather surprised to be joining in the laughter and the jokes, even though he was not too sure what was going on.

After a couple of hours of this, James noticed that Thomas was becoming decidedly sleepy and thought it was time that they make their way home. There were enough willing hands to help him get his half-brother out into the fresh air, but the only way that James could get the now mostly insensible Thomas to stay on his horse was by draping him head down across the saddle, like a dead hero returning from battle.

So they arrived home. Thomas' stepmother had been watching from an upper window. When eventually she saw the two horses approaching, she rushed to her husband's study.

'I fear something terrible has overtaken your son. James is bringing him home and he is lying across his horse. There must have been a terrible accident.'

Both concerned parents rushed to the main door just as James arrived, leading his brother's horse. His mother let out a terrible cry as James leapt down and pulled the still mostly unconscious Thomas off his horse.

'I'm sorry father. I tried to stop him but he would insist on going to the inn.'

There is that strange trait in all of us, that when our worst fears are found to be baseless, we turn to anger instead of relief. So it was now with Sir Walter.

'The boy's drunk!' he bellowed.

Recognising his father's voice, Thomas shook himself free of his brother's arm, smiled idiotically at the assembled people, took a few stumbling steps forward, then collapsed onto his knees and was promptly sick on his father's leather shoes.

Sir Walter was so incensed that he was determined to disinherit his elder son immediately. As luck would have it, the noted lawyer Sir Egremont Thynne, his wife's brother, was staying in the house at the time and he was happy to draft the necessary documents. Thomas was able to say nothing in his defence; in fact, that afternoon, if someone had approached him with a loaded pistol, he would have been happy to take it out of their hands and put himself out of his misery.

Sir Egremont's clerk was fetched, who could turn the draft into a proper legal document (to engross it, to use the technical term). That would mean sitting up all night to complete the work. As he was writing by the light of a candle, he thought he saw a shadow on the parchment. When he looked up he saw a hand reaching for his quill. He gave a start but when he looked again, the hand had vanished.

Thinking it merely his fancy and the result of working too long into the night, he went back to his writing but again a long white hand, surely that of a woman, came into his vision, reaching out as if to stop his pen; but once again, it vanished as soon as he looked directly at it.

Now badly shaken, it was several minutes before the clerk could steel himself to start up the copying again. As soon as he did so, he saw the hand again and this time he had the distinct impression that it was reaching out to grab his own hand. He had dropped his quill and was out of that room faster than ever he had moved in his life before.

He was down the stairs and into his riding coat before anything could stop him. He stayed long enough to tell the astonished servants what had befallen him, and that no reward on this earth would get him to go back into that room. Then he was out into the night and to the stables, where he got on his horse and put as many miles as he could between himself and the house.

Sir Egremont was fetched from his sleep, and the strange goings on explained to him. However, he was made of stronger stuff than his clerk and angrily went into the room and completed the document. If he was troubled by any spectral appearance, he never spoke of it afterwards. So the new will was ready for Sir Walter Long to sign and seal by daybreak, which he happily did.

Sadly Sir Walter did not live very long after these occurrences. Whether this was because if his general ill health, disappointment at the actions of his son or that his wife did not want time to mellow his displeasure, it would be impossible to say. However, he was not going to go quietly to his grave. The clerk had been so disturbed by the events of that night that he went to the Pakingtons and told them that their daughter's son was in danger of losing his birth rights. They were incensed, and were intent on doing something about it. Naturally they turned to the law.

When Sir Walter's body was carried to his funeral it was arrested at the church porch by officials appointed by the Pakingtons. A massive court case followed, that made quite a few lawyers' fortunes. In the end it was decided that the estate be split in two, so that both young men should have sufficient estate to maintain himself as a gentleman. Thomas learned of his mother's intervention and was forever grateful, and did all he could to honour her memory. He never went into a tavern again.

EIGHTEEN

FOLEY THE FIDDLER

Boundary changes are a great curse. The town of Stourbridge has historically been counted as part of Worcestershire, but some bureaucrat thought recently to break that centuries-old arrangement and move it into the West Midlands. As an act of defiance to this breaking of tradition, I include this story that, since its origins in the seventeenth century, has been taken as a story of Worcestershire.

Richard Foley thought he had the best job in the world. He was a fiddler. He also had a small bit of land and a cottage, enough to support a wife and a cow but the hard work that it demanded, he gave grudgingly. He preferred taking his fiddle and going down to one of the local inns or taverns of Stourbridge and playing for whoever was there. In return, he was paid what few coins the people could spare, quite a bit of beer and, best of all, the laughter and joy he saw on the faces of the people as he played.

Stourbridge was richly endowed with all the resources needed to smelt iron, and many of the people for whom he played were involved in this or the nail making business, nails being vital to many other trades. In the taverns he would listen to the nail-makers and hear what a hard task it was, and he thanked Providence that he was a fiddle player, rather than being involved in the nail trade.

He heard especially what labour and time was lost in the arduous work of dividing the rods of iron so that they could be made into nails. He also listened to the curses that were heaped on the heads of the Swedes, who had recently discovered a process called slitting that made the whole thing faster and easier, so that Swedish nails were now cheaper and threatened to destroy the Stourbridge men's living.

One afternoon he was in a tavern as usual, playing his fiddle and having partaken of more than his fair share of good English ale, when his wife burst through the door, ashen faced.

'I knew I would find you here, you wastrel!' she bellowed. Richard stopped in the middle of a jig, this time annoyed by the laughter all around him.

'The bailiff's come for our cow because you can't pay the rent. What are we going to do now?'

Richard considered this for a time. He realised that his good life was over and he was going to have to find another. Slowly and deliberately he stood up.

'I'm sorry wife, I can do nothing for you. Sell what you can and see what a life you can make for yourself with it.'

With that, he walked out of the door carrying his fiddle and was seen no more in his old haunts. Opinion was divided in the town of Stourbridge as to his fate. Some thought he had gone to London to seek his fortune, others that he had thrown himself into the River Stour.

In fact he had done neither of those things. He had walked north-east until he came to the port of Hull and from there taken a ship to Uppsala, the centre of the Swedish iron trade, paying his way with his fiddle tunes. Once there he begged and fiddled his way about the place. The Swedes took him to their hearts. He spoke no Swedish, and although eventually he did pick up a few words – they could see that he was a bit slow. Things needed explaining to him several times, and even then, he quickly seemed to forget them and they had to be explained yet again. Still, they enjoyed his new English tunes and were prepared to put up with his lack of intelligence for his fast fingers and bow.

Eventually he found his way to Dannemora, the site of one of those new slitting mills. While the industrious Swedes would sweat and labour in the mill, Foley would play his fiddle and watch what was going on. The mill owners did not mind this; in fact they rather liked Foley paying some of his fast dance tunes because it seemed to encourage their men to work harder. The Englishman was polite and tried to take an interest in what they were doing there, but could not seem to take it in. In fact it became something of a joke; them smiling, taking him through the process, and him, smiling, trying to follow but often getting it wrong so they would have to start again.

Three years passed, and most people in Stourbridge had forgotten that a man called Richard Foley had ever existed, when he turned up again. But he did not visit his old haunts; instead he went to see Mr Knight, one of the biggest iron founders in the district, and told him that he had discovered the Swedish secret of slitting. Naturally, Knight was sceptical that this ne'er-do-well had anything useful to show him, but Richard was eventually able to convince him, through drawings and explanation, that he actually knew what he was talking about.

Using Knight's money and expertise, the necessary buildings and machinery were built. At last, the great day came when iron could be quickly and cheaply split in England. The machine was set in motion and it completely failed to split the iron. Knight looked angrily at Foley, who looked shocked and dumbfounded. Some of the workmen laughed openly at him. Splitting the iron by hand might be hard work, but at least it was a living. They were a bit worried that this new process would take that away from them.

Foley disappeared again and this time people were agreed that he must have thrown himself into the Stour out of shame. But Richard Foley had been used to worse embarrassments in his life, and he was not so easily made despondent. He set off back to Sweden to find out where he had gone wrong.

His old friends were delighted by his return. So much so that, having nowhere else to stay, they allowed him to sleep in the mill overnight. There he was able to make more careful measurements than he had been able to before. Having stayed just long enough to make sure he had rectified the mistakes he had made previously, he disappeared once again.

His reappearance in Stourbridge was greeted with less enthusiasm than his earlier return but, his explanations sounding plausible and the rewards of success so great, he was provided with the wherewithal to construct a second mill. This proved successful, and from being a poor fiddler, Richard Foley was set to become one of the richest men in the kingdom. Thanks to him, Stourbridge became the centre of the nail-making industry in Britain, but there was a price. In order to become successful, the once easy going fellow had to become as hard in business as his nails.

When he died, Richard Foley, once a poor fiddler, was buried in the place of honour in Oldswinford church, just below the chancel steps. His family went into politics, one of them becoming Speaker of the House of Commons. Naturally, they became even richer. They did not like the idea that their fortune was founded by an industrial spy or worse, a wastrel. They put it about that Richard had been quite well-to-do, more like a commercial traveller than a tavern-haunter, and the fiddling story was just some folk tale that never happened and, if it did, then it was about some other family altogether. The family built two huge mansions; one at Great Witley, and the other at Stoke Edith in Herefordshire. Strangely both were later destroyed by fire. Perhaps someone in Sweden put their other important industry to good use; that of making matches.

NINETEEN

THE BATTLE OF WORCESTER

The English Civil War started and ended in Worcestershire. In 1642 the first bloodletting was at the Battle of Powick Bridge. Nine long years later, the final battle would be fought over much the same ground at the Battle of Worcester.

In reality the Battle of Powick Bridge was little more than a skirmish, although it was pretty important to the men who were killed in it. Two squadrons of cavalry, one Royalist, one for Parliament, had unbeknownst to each other, camped in neighbouring fields one night. It was the Royalist cavalry that got up earliest, and realising the danger, attacked the Parliamentarians before they were fully aware of the situation and sent them galloping for their lives.

By 1651 Charles I and many of his subjects were dead. His son, the future Charles II, had now allied himself with the Scots, who had previously fought on the side of Parliament. War can be a confusing thing. His experienced army commander, Leslie, wanted to stay in Scotland and fight Cromwell on home territory, but Charles knew he would never be King of England if he did not control London, so ordered the army south.

He expected to literally steal a march on Cromwell and be in London before the fellow could catch up with him. However, either through informers or supernatural skill, Cromwell discovered the plan and was hot on his heels. Charles knew he would now never reach London before the Parliamentary army that outnumbered his own by two to one would catch up with him, so he turned his force to the west, a region he hoped would still be sympathetic to him, and where he could get reinforcements.

The King's army arrived in Worcester on 25 August. It had been a terrible journey, through the heat of an unusually warm August. The generals faced a difficult dilemma; to drag the army on, or to rest and prepare to meet the enemy at Worcester. They decided to stay, and set about digging defensive ditches and emplacements around the east of the city, the direction Cromwell was coming from.

A few days later the Parliamentary army duly arrived, but it did not attack straight away. Instead it waited, giving the Royalists more time to prepare. Why did an experienced general like Cromwell do such a thing? Some say he was preparing pontoon bridges by which to quickly cross the rivers when the time came. Others say that he was waiting until the auspicious date of 3 September; a year before, on that day, he had won a magnificent victory at Dunbar and was being a little superstitious. Others say that his hesitation was because of an altogether more sinister reason.

On the evening of 2 September, Cromwell was sitting in his tent with one of his senior commanders, Colonel Lindsey. Lindsey later recalled that his friend seemed very distracted that evening, but put that down to the terrible test they would both face the next day; the battle that would decide the fate of the nation.

As dusk approached, Cromwell suddenly sat up, as if he had heard something. For a moment it looked as if he was listening intently, than he abruptly stood up. 'Come, Lindsey.' He called and walked out of the tent. The Colonel had to run to catch up, as Cromwell walked quickly to his horse and mounted.

They rode to a nearby wood. Lindsey was concerned. He did not feel it right that his commander should be exposing himself to such risk. Without saying anything, Cromwell dismounted and walked into the wood. Lindsey did likewise, but as soon as he entered the great darkness, he started to feel uneasy. He was a seasoned soldier and had faced many dangers, but now the hackles of his neck were rising. It was as if the forest was cloaked in some terrible dread.

He found himself hanging back, but Cromwell pushed determinedly ahead. They came to a clearing, and while Lindsey hid in the shadows, Cromwell paced up and down in the centre. In a little while, an elderly man dressed in black came out from under the trees on the opposite side of the clearing. He was carrying a parchment which Cromwell snatched from him and read, as Lindsey had seen him read many an urgent dispatch.

'This is only for seven years!' cried Cromwell. 'I asked for twenty-one.'

The old man shook his head. 'My master says it is for seven, nothing more.'

'At least give me fourteen.'

'It's seven or nothing.'

'Very well then, let it be so,' angrily, Cromwell thrust the document back into the old man's hands and strode back the way he had come. He saw Lindsey lurking by a tree, looking shocked, as if he had completely forgotten the man's presence. But he quickly collected himself and clapped the man on his shoulder.

'Good news Lindsey. We shall have victory tomorrow.'

And so it proved. The initial Parliamentary attack at Powick Bridge was repulsed by the battle-hardened Scots but Cromwell used his pontoon bridges to cross the Severn and Teme, and outflank the Royalist army who broke and ran. Three thousand men were killed, mostly Royalists in the ensuing rout. Charles, in Worcester, saw all was lost and also ran for it, given time by his bodyguard selling their lives dearly. He escaped from the city hidden in a cart. As well as his army, Charles left behind a tailors' bill of £453 3s for uniforms – it was not paid by the Royal Family until 2008.

Despite a high price on his head, he eventually reached France, having needed at various times to dress as a woman and hide up an oak tree in Boscobel Park to evade his pursuers. His army was not so lucky. Cromwell conscripted 3,000 English prisoners into his army and sent them to the terrible war then raging in Ireland. The 8,000 captured Scots fared even less well, being sent to work the plantations of the West Indies as virtual slaves.

Lindsey returned to his native Norfolk, his heart deeply troubled by what he had witnessed the night before the battle. Eventually he told his minister, Mr Thorowgood and told him he was certain that Cromwell would die seven years after Worcester.

Cromwell's rule did not go nearly as well as many people had hoped. Perhaps the expectations were just too high, as they were for a Prime Minister nearer our own day, although Blair stands accused of supping with American devils rather than those from Hell.

In August 1658, Cromwell suddenly fell ill. After a rapid decline he died on Friday 3 September, exactly seven years after the Battle of Worcester. He was believed to have died from septicaemia, caused by the mishandling of a urinary complaint by his doctors. Shortly before his death, a terrible storm hit the south of the country, uprooting trees and with a west wind so strong, that according to one of Cromwell's own generals, Edmund Ludlow, 'the horses were not able to draw against it.' People later decided it must have been caused by the Devil dragging Cromwell down to Hell. No doubt Colonel Lindsey agreed with them.

In 1660, eighteen years after the Battle of Powick Bridge and nine years after Worcester, Charles II was restored to the throne. On 30 January 1661, the twelfth anniversary of the execution of Charles I, Cromwell's body was exhumed from Westminster Abbey and dragged to Tyburn, where it was hanged in chains. Afterwards the head was cut off and the body thrown into a common burial pit. The head was stuck on a pole and exhibited outside Westminster Hall where it stayed until 1685.

TWENTY

THE EVESHAM WITCH

On their own the children of Evesham were a well-behaved bunch. Seeing them in church, seated next to their parents, you would have thought them as godly and incapable of mischief as any child in Christendom. At home they did their chores without complaint and did not speak until they were spoken to.

It was a different story when they went out in a gang. Their parents had to work hard for a living and could not be expected to keep an eye on them all the time. So when the opportunity arose, they went out to cause mayhem.

One Saturday spring morning a group of them told their mothers they were going out into the fields to gather cowslips. Glad to have them out from under their feet, the women happily assented to this harmless pastime. But, out of sight of their cottages, their children had a different sport in mind.

They were a group of girls mostly aged about twelve or thirteen, that difficult age, which is neither child nor young woman. The youngest of them, nine-year-old Mary Ellins, the daughter of Edward Ellins, a gardener, was only allowed to come with them on sufferance; if no other game presented itself, they could always torment her.

They went, not to the fields, but to Catherine Huxley's poor cottage. Catherine was an unfortunate soul of about forty with no husband or son to protect her. A hard life had given her an uncertain temper so she was easy to bait.

When they got to the hovel they found they were out of luck. They looked through the window but there was no one in the single room that was Catherine's home. Disappointed, they debated what to do; perhaps they would have to go and pick cowslips after all.

Then Mary, not involved in the discussion, spotted a movement out of the corner of her eye. There was Catherine Huxley, crouching in the ditch. Her cottage had no privy so she had to make whatever arrangements she could.

'Look,' Mary said to the other girls and pointed.

'There she is,' they cried and then, 'Witch! Witch!'

One of the oldest girls picked up a stone and threw it at Catherine. It missed but another threw with better aim. Soon a

volley of stones was flying at the unfortunate woman. In desperation Catherine stood up and started to get out of the ditch.
The girls screamed, and giggling and laughing, turned and ran;
all but Mary. She had not been expecting the stone throwing
and now stood rooted to the spot, unable to do anything but
look at the approaching figure.

Something cracked inside Catherine. 'Ellins!' she cried, 'You
shall have stones enough when you piss!'

This broke the spell. Mary turned and ran as fast as she
could. She ran home, flustered and scared.

'Where are your cowslips, Mary?' asked her mother, but all
Mary could do was burst into tears.

'Have those big girls been teasing you again?' asked her
mother, but all Mary wanted to do was hide her face in her
mother's skirts.

That afternoon Mary started to come down with a fever. Her
mother was anxious and watched over her. A fever could take a
child in days. Mary complained of a pain in her back, as if she
was being pricked by pins. Then she needed to relieve herself and
started to scream with the pain. There was a clink, and when her
mother looked, there was a small pebble in the bottom of the pot
and Mary was whimpering as small children do when the worst
of the pain is over but not completely gone away.

There was another pebble the next time she needed to relieve
herself; this time a small piece of flint. And another and another
throughout the day, and each time Mary screamed so loud that
she brought the neighbours round. Mrs Ellins at first accused
Mary of eating pebbles and said that this was the consequence,
but Mary swore she had not done so, and as one of the neighbours said, if that had been the case they would have come out
the other end.

At last Mary told them of her encounter with Catherine Huxley and what the woman had said to her. The Justice of the Peace was sent for. He listened to the child's testimony and he examined the stones. By now there were almost eighty of them. Some were pebbles, some flints; some small, some about an ounce in weight.

Then he went to Catherine's house with half a dozen tough men, and for safety's sake, the local minister. Despite the woman's protestations of innocence they took the place apart, visions of the unfortunate little girl in their minds and righteous indignation in their hearts. It did not take long to search the one-roomed cottage. Nothing was found until one man looked under the bed. There he found a pile of stones, very like the ones that had come out of Mary. That was enough to arrest Catherine and get her dragged to Worcester Gaol.

She was tried at the summer Assizes in the city. There were two damning pieces of evidence: the pebbles found underneath her bed – for which she had no explanation – and the fact that, as soon as her arrest was known, little Mary stopped passing the stones, voiding only blackish and muddy sand instead. She was found guilty and hanged.

Young Mary soon made a perfect recovery. But she and her stones were now famous. The family were plagued by the gentry coming to gawp, some offering to buy some of the stones; but the family did not consider that such a thing was right. In the end they told anyone who asked that they had been buried. Mary grew up with no signs of being affected by her bewitchment. Eventually she would marry and have children of her own, though she always kept an eye on them when they said they were going out to pick cowslips.

Although the family declared that none of the stones were in circulation, that did not prevent many pebbles being sold as the authentic material that had passed through Mary Ellins. One of these was acquired by Thomas Wriothesley (pronounced Risley), Earl of Southampton. He had supported Charles I in the recent unpleasantness, but had not taken up arms against Parliament and had been allowed to stay in the country on payment of a large fine.

Despite his wealth and importance he was terribly afflicted with the kidney stones. Driven to distraction by the pain, he was even more terrified of the surgeon's knife and was forever looking for alternative cures, such as the Ellins stone. This he had ground down, and he drank it dissolved in a glass of wine. Sadly it did him no good.

When Charles II returned to the throne Thomas was appointed Lord High Treasurer of England, one of the most important positions in the country; a post in which he was remarkably honest but somewhat incompetent.

He continued to search for cures for his condition. Eventually he heard of an old lady who lived just the other side of respectability, and with her dealings with spirits and knowledge of hidden skills, would be sure to cure him. He sent his agent to acquire a suitable potion that would dissolve the stones. As soon as he had it in his possession, he greedily drank it down and then let out a terrible scream, as if he had swallowed acid. He was in torment for several hours until merciful death came to claim him.

TWENTY ONE

THE UPTON GHOST

Captain Thomas Bound was one of the wickedest men who ever lived, at least according to the people of Upton-on-Severn. They should know, because he lived amongst them during the middle part of the seventeenth century. Mind you, they were a little biased. While most of them supported the King during the bitter Civil War, Thomas Bound was for Parliament, and was not afraid of letting people know it. As a churchwarden he took against the popular rector William Woodforde, whom he despised for the man's supposed Papist sympathies, and connived at his removal. If that was not bad enough, he was strongly suspected of moving some boundary markers on the productive riverside meadow known as The Ham, thereby enlarging his property. Everyone knew that any man who moved boundary markers was cursed; it said so in the Bible. The people of Upton-on-Severn kept a wary eye on Thomas Bound, who was described as a grim and covetous man.

As a young man he had married a local girl called Mary. For a few months they seemed blissfully happy, but then Mary sickened and died. Just a few months later Bound found himself another Mary, this time from a few villages off, and married her.

When she too died within a few months of the marriage people put two and two together and noticed that Thomas Bound had done pretty well out of both marriage settlements. Then, a few years later, he took a third wife, this one called Margaret, from a bit further off. The villagers watched her health with a great deal of interest. Perhaps because of that she remained fit and healthy.

During the Civil War he was absent from the village, and many people thought that it was the best thing about the fighting. They rather hoped he would stop a musket ball or have some like tragedy befall him. However, he returned with a vengeance in 1651. Upton was a strategic site, having the only bridge on the Severn between Worcester and Gloucester. It was defended by a strong Royalist force under Major General Massey, but an even stronger army, led by Cromwell himself, was approaching from the east, intent on reaching Worcester and capturing Charles II.

Under cover of darkness eighteen brave parliamentary soldiers forded the Severn, seized the church and were able to hold it until reinforcements could cross the bridge. From there Cromwell was able to march on Worcester and, as we have seen in one of the stories above, end the fighting. Although Bound was not one of the volunteers, he was suspected locally of advising Cromwell about the lay of the land and he now boasted the rank of Captain, something he insisted the villagers call him at every opportunity. Even after the return of the king, Bound's devilish luck held and he was able to hold on to all his riches, although he did have to put up with the return of Parson Woodforde.

But in 1667 he overreached himself. The Bromleys were an old Upton family and for many years had been the major landowners in the area. They had been supportive of the Parliamentary cause, but had not been as lucky as

Captain Bound and the family was now reduced to one local representative: old Mrs Bromley. While Bound lived in a fine house called Soley's Orchard, he also leased a larger one, Southend Farm, from Mrs Bromley.

When Bound heard that Mrs Bromley had fallen seriously ill he went, as a good neighbour should, to visit her and see if he could be of assistance in any way. He found her much agitated, because she felt death approaching and had not made a will. She particularly wanted to leave Southend Farm to her last remaining relative, a nephew who lived in London. Bound readily agreed to help her make the will and guided her hand over the paper to her dictation. Unfortunately, when it came to putting in the name of the beneficiary, he helped her write his name instead of the nephew's.

A few days later poor Mrs Bromley died, the will was discovered and Captain Bound took ownership of Southend Farm. But things did not go well for him. Perhaps it was his guilty conscience, or perhaps Mrs Bromley, with the clear sight of the dead, discovered that she had been cheated. She took to haunting Thomas Bound, appearing at any time of the day or night and looking at him with a reproachful stare that turned his blood to water. He felt that he was never free of her. Sometimes it would be that a day or two would go by without him seeing her and he thought he might have got away with it, but then she would turn up again and might stay for the whole night, or sit in front of him at mealtimes.

In the end he could stand it no longer. In late July his body was found floating face down in a pool by the Causeway, a raised path that ran between Southend and Rectory Road. Mrs Bromley was seen no more, now being able to go to her eternal rest. The same could not be said for Captain Bound.

Now his ghost started appearing at night around Soley's Orchard, Southend and Rectory Road. If the people of Upton had no liking for Thomas Bound when he was alive, they liked him even less now that he was dead and scaring the wits out of them. They decided he would have to be done away with a second time and asked the vicar to do something about it.

The clergyman had read a few books on the subject, so he thought he knew what to do. He took a 1in length of beeswax candle down to the pool. He lit it and read the Service of Commination (look it up in the Book of Common Prayer) over the water and then threw the candle into the pool, ordering Bound to be quiet until it was relit. Sadly, this proved ineffective. Indeed, it made things a damned sight worse, because the ghost seemed to have gained some power from the ceremony and now started appearing in daylight as well as the dark.

In desperation the vicar went to see the Bishop of Worcester, who sent him back with two other clergymen more skilled in the art of exorcism. They held the ceremony in the cellar at Soley's Orchard. Protected by a circle of salt and each carrying a Bible and a lighted candle, they summoned the spirit with the intention of forcing it to drown itself in the Red Sea. As they said the words of summoning, they felt the atmosphere in the cellar change. It was getting colder and they felt they were no longer alone. The vicar of Upton was so overwrought that he stepped outside the circle. Instantly there was a sound like fat sizzling in a frying pan and something hot hit him on the cheek. It was said after that no hair would ever grow on that spot again. The clergymen very quickly got out of the cellar and it was bricked up, but despite this, Bound's ghost was soon seen again, sitting on a stone by the pool where he had met his end. He was also seen walking up Rectory Lane with a land-measuring chain clanking behind him. He also developed a habit of appearing out of the early morning mist to any fisherman who was foolhardy enough to be fishing on the banks of the Severn at such an ungodly hour. Some people also claimed to have seen the ghosts of his three wives with him, which might account for why he appeared so miserable when he manifested himself.

So it went on for many years. With the coming of the railways Soley's Orchard was demolished because it stood in the way of the line and that seemed to lessen Bound's haunting. In the mid-nineteenth century it was decided to modernise Upton church, and in the course of the restoration, Bound's grave was discovered in the chancel. Surprisingly that too seemed to lessen his appearances. It is said that one of the workmen stole the skull and used it as a drinking vessel. If that is true then he was a braver man than I am.

Although Bound's manifestations became less frequent, they did not stop altogether. In the 1930s he so badly frightened a police inspector who had gone down Rectory Road to investigate a disturbance that the case made headline news in the national papers.

The bad news is that Captain Thomas Bound's ghost has still not been laid. When a sheep or cow gets out on the road, causing chaos, the people of Upton close their doors with a cry of, 'Here he comes again!'

So, if you happen to be walking down Rectory Road late at night and you hear some strange clanking behind you, don't, whatever you do, turn round.

THE MURDEROUS VICAR OF BROUGHTON HACKETT

On the whole vicars of the Church of England do sterling work and most of them assiduously avoid breaking any of the Ten Commandments. Unfortunately, Revd James Lee, the vicar of St Leonards in Broughton Hackett during the time of Queen Anne, broke most of them – including the really important ones.

He started out in a small way, with some light blaspheming and not being particularly careful of how he spent his time between services on a Sunday. But, as all too many of us know, such small acorns of peccadilloes have an unfortunate likelihood of growing into whopping great oaks.

One Sunday he was seated outside the local hostelry, having partaken of a meal that would have kept a pauper in good fettle for several months, and enough beer to baptise an infant. His somewhat unfocused gaze drifted to a horse being ridden past and from it to its rider, whom he saw was a young woman of surprising beauty. He watched her bobbing down the road with interest.

'Who was that?' he asked, casually.

'Oh, that was old Sam Taylor's wife. Him that keeps Chequers Farm,' replied his drinking companion. He digested the information, along with another pint of beer.

It struck him that night, as he lay awake in his bed, that the vicarage was a damnably lonely place. It also struck him that he had not been as careful as he should have been in his pastoral visits to outlying farms and resolved to correct the matter the following morning. With that he fell asleep, blissfully unthinking of the tenth commandment, the one about coveting.

For once in his life he kept to his good intention, and rode off the next morning to pay a call at Chequers Farm. The farmer's wife proved as good-looking close up as he had thought her from a distance and seemed genuinely pleased to see him. The farmer, not unexpectedly, was absent on farm business, so the vicar was able to spend a long hour discoursing with the young woman. He, who knew his Chaucer, deduced that this was a typical May and Januarie marriage, in which the wife felt unfulfilled in several departments.

Over the next few months he continued paying court to Mrs Taylor under the guise of parish visits. He was a clever one and increased his visits to many of his other parishioners as well. They were quite astounded in the change in the man. Being university educated and something of a charmer in his youth, and she a simple farmer's daughter unused to the ways of the world, it was not too long before Revd James Lee's stratagems paid off and the two were breaking the seventh commandment on a reasonably regular basis.

Now, it is often the fault of the young to underestimate the thought processes of their elders. Even to a busy and much put-upon farmer it gradually became obvious that his wife had changed in some mysterious way. She no longer seemed as grateful as she had once been that he had taken her in, put a roof over her head and provided her with what fancies and fairings as a man in his position could be expected to provide. Where once there had been softness, there now was scratching and grating. Since he thought himself the good fellow he had always been, he came to the conclusion that any man would and took to keeping a closer but surreptitious watch on his wife. Thus he discovered how assiduous the parson was being in his pastoral visits and his wrath, as it says in the Bible, was greatly kindled.

One Sunday the reverend rushed through Matins in order to visit his paramour, but when he reached the farm, he found not his lady but her husband waiting for him at the farmhouse door, arms on hips, watching him come up the path. Disappointed but sensing a little tension in the air, the parson resolved to be as civil as he could.

'Good day sir. Your sheep are looking well. They will make you a fair price at market I imagine.'

'Don't try any of your soft-soap with me, you blackguard. If you are looking for the baggage, you won't find her. I've sent her back to her mother's. As for you, I'm off to see the bishop. See what he makes of a vicar whose morals would disgrace a polecat.'

Reverend Lee's face went white. His stomach lurched and pictures of ruin and penury flashed through his mind. All he could think of was how to avert this tragedy. His eyes fell on a mattock by the door, which the farmer had been using to do some weeding while he waited for the vicar to put in an appearance. Lee seized it and swung it with desperate force at his tormentor. The blade hit Sam Taylor on the side of the head and he fell, poleaxed. He twitched a bit and then lay still.

Lee watched with horror as the blood oozed onto the path, soaking into the earth. For what seemed like an age he just stood there, unable to move. Then a new wave of desperation flowed down his back like cold water. He knew he must get rid of the body, but how? He turned right, he turned left, he turned back down the path by which he had arrived, as if his feet wanted to be away from this terrible place. Then his eyes caught sight of the bakehouse, a separate small brick structure by the side of the farmhouse, and his thoughts turned to the large oven in there.

He started to drag the body towards it but this left a great smear of blood along the path, so he went inside the farmhouse and fetched the sheet off the bed, wrapped the farmer in it and then proceeded, with several stops to regain his strength, towards the bakehouse. It took him all that afternoon to complete his task, getting the fire lit and bringing it up to a sufficient temperature for his purpose. While the body was being consumed in the flames he cleaned the path as best he could. Then he removed the ashes, crushing the skull and the larger bones that had remained intact, and then disposing of them down the cesspit. It was the hardest day's work he had ever done, and by the time he returned to the vicarage, he was exhausted and in a fever. He sent word to the church warden that he was too ill to take evensong that night.

He slept remarkably well, and then spent the week swinging from elation that he had got away with it to horror at the enormity of his crime. No news came from the farm, so he assumed that nothing untoward had been discovered. As Sunday approached Lee found that he had a fear of entering the dark sanctity of St Leonard's, but knew that he dare not avoid taking the service for fear of arousing suspicion. On entering the building he almost expected to be struck down, but when nothing happened, he carried on with preparations for the service, appearing as if nothing was wrong but inwardly gripped by a feeling of unease.

Unbeknownst to the vicar, the farmer had a twin brother. He lived in Warwickshire, so the two had not seen each other for some time. The previous Sunday he had been enjoying his dinner when a terrible pain struck him in the head. As this subsided he was seized by the certainty that something terrible had happened to his brother. He was in business, so could not drop everything immediately, but by the Saturday, had got his affairs in sufficient order that he could make the journey to Broughton Hackett.

It was the middle of the Sunday morning by the time he reached his brother's farm. His worries were not abated by finding the place completely deserted. He was wondering what to do when he heard the bells of St Leonard's ringing out across the countryside. Relieved and thinking that his brother and wife must be there, he set off in that direction.

Revd James Lee was in the pulpit, composing himself for his sermon. There was silence in the church as his parishioners waited. Suddenly the latch of the south door cracked in the quiet church like a musket bullet and the wooden door creaked open.

Some turned to look at the intruder, but those polite people who remained looking at the vicar saw his face freeze with horror. For what Revd Lee saw coming through the doorway was the ghost of the man he had murdered. As the spectre walked down the aisle towards him he let out a terrified scream and collapsed on the pulpit floor.

The congregation erupted into chaos. Some of them laid hands on the brother and demanded what he had done to their vicar while others tried to stop them, saying it was only old Sam Taylor; still others ran and dragged the unfortunate vicar down the pulpit steps and started slapping his face as a method of bringing him back to his senses. This was eventually successful, but as Lee regained consciousness, he found he could not bear to keep his secret any longer. He babbled out his crime to the shock of his parishioners and the distress of the man from Warwickshire.

The people of Broughton Hackett are a proud people. They did not look forward to the scandal that must shortly engulf them. The squire, the curate and a few of the larger farmers, as well as the aggrieved brother, met in secret session. A bold and daring plan was agreed upon. The squire wrote to the bishop, explaining that Lee had tragically died and that he favoured the appointment of the curate as replacement. As for the man himself, it was left to the brother to decide what to do with him. Unfortunately for Lee, he was a vindictive man.

The parson was shut in an iron cage and suspended from a large oak tree near Churchill Mill. Next to him was suspended another cage with a good quantity of food and drink, just out of reach. There he was left, until he starved to death.

The curate, or rather the new vicar, was an honest man. He wrote the details of the affair down in the parish register and, over the years, new incumbents were told but also warned never to breathe a word of it. In the course of time, the powers that be decided that all the parish registers must be centralised and brought together in one place. Now, if you doubt the truth of my story, go and ask to see the parish register of Broughton Hackett. You will find the pages for this period of Queen Anne's reign mysteriously torn out.

CRABBING THE PARSON

Unfortunate vicars having to cover several widely spread parishes on a Sunday is not an altogether recent phenomenon. This was the fate of the Revd John Clerk at the beginning of the eighteenth century, whose living included both Frankley and Romsley churches.

Although they kept him busy, they were but poor livings, so the reverend had quite a hard time of it keeping body and soul together and had no spare cash for indulgences such as a wife and children.

One hot Sunday in July he was walking from Frankley, where he had said Matins, to Romsley, where he would give the afternoon service. Dressed in his clerical black suit and tight collar, the sun beat down upon him mercilessly and he was tempted to change his sermon to an extemporisation on the Book of Job. But he knew he could not, for this was the Sunday nearest 28 July – St Kenelm's Day. St Kenelm was the popular local saint, and his congregation would expect a description of the wretched child's beheading and a discourse on how they should be inspired by his fate to lead good and saintly lives.

It came to midday, when the sun was at its fiercest, so Revd Clerk decided to take his dinner. He dropped his knapsack from off his back and sat down in the shade of a tree beside the road. Just as he could not afford a horse to make his journey easier, so he could not afford to stop for splendid meals at a wayside inn as many of his colleagues, with richer livings, could afford to do. He carefully unwrapped a sacking parcel from his canonicals. This contained his lunch; some bread and cheese.

The bread was dry and the cheese was drier. The weight of a bottle of water had been too much for his back. As he ate, the parson meditated on the joys of leading a blameless life. His eyes rose up to heaven, but all he saw was more pitiless blue sky. He became aware that he was sitting opposite an apple orchard. On the tree nearest to him, bobbing on a branch in a carefree manner, was one perfectly ripe apple.

Clerk had not tasted an apple since last autumn, when they had been plentiful. Now his dry mouth longed to taste the sweet juice of that fruit. He was the representative of the Anglican Church, which believed in property rights as strongly as it believed in the Trinity; yet the unfortunate priest could not take his eyes off the soft, red, luscious apple dancing so provocatively above him.

This was the land of William Tomkins, a local farmer who also acted as churchwarden for Romsley. Surely he would not begrudge his vicar an apple? He paid his tithes every year. This would only be a small foretaste of that tax. Revd Clerk had never scrumped an apple in his life; he had been a much too well behaved boy for such a thing, but now he found himself standing up and planning his navigation up the tree.

He looked guiltily around him but the lane was empty. Driven by his thirst he repacked and buckled his knapsack for a quick getaway and then shinned up the tree. After three attempts at grabbing the apple as it bobbed in the air, he kept a judicious hold of the tree with one hand and finally held its gentle flesh. He tugged, and it was his. Hastily he slithered back down the tree, his prize held securely.

He returned to his former position, sat down and was about the take that first wonderful bite when he heard footsteps approaching, and a hundred yards behind him there was the dratted figure of Tomkins the farmer coming round the corner. Quickly he looked around. His knapsack was buckled and he had no intention of just throwing his booty into the hedgerow. His only option was to drop the apple down his coat sleeve. Then he watched the farmer approach with his head in his hand, in what he hoped was a contemplative gesture.

'Afternoon, parson,' said the farmer.

'Good day, Mr Tomkins.'

The farmer paused to look at his fields in a content, proprietorial sort of way. Then he looked at the apple tree.

'Damnation, someone's stolen my apple! I was looking forward to that after my dinner. I bet it was that little Billy Foster. I'll warm his backside for this, the torrell.'

He looked for sympathy to the Revd Clerk and found the parson blushing mightily, so unused was he to the ways of sin. He took a longer look at the strange way he was sitting.

'I suppose we better be off to the church,' he said.

'You go on Mr Tomkins. I'll just contemplate this fine view a moment longer.'

'Well, I'll just sit here with you then.' The farmer sat down opposite the parson and watched him closely.

Clerk saw no option but to get to his feet and, still keeping his arm straight and upright, slipped his knapsack onto his back.

'Mustn't hold you up, Mr Tomkins. Perhaps we can proceed at a slow pace. This warmth precludes rush I think.'

So they walked together to Romsley church. The farmer's discourse seemed mostly to turn to the topic of apples, while the parson tried to take it otherwise. Even when they reached the church Clerk found no solace, because the farmer kept an eye on him while they prepared for the service. The unfortunate fellow had to go through some wild contortions to get his vestments on successfully.

Romsley might boast quite a small church but it did, in those days, have a magnificent double-decker pulpit, with the vicar in splendour at the top, towering over his congregation, and the clerk below him. Reverend Clerk and Mr Tomkins took their respective stations. The Revd Clerk had no problem during the hymns or the Bible readings, although he did have to contort himself a bit during the prayers. The apple had become a great burden to him and lay in his sleeve like the weight of sin.

However, he prided himself on being an inspiring preacher, and this proved his undoing. Describing the tragedy of

St Kenelm to the assembly, he became animated and started throwing his arms about to illustrate the cruelty heaped onto the head of the unfortunate saint. During one of these manoeuvres his arms flew downwards and the apple became dislodged from its hiding position. It plummeted down and hit the head of Mr Tomkins.

He had been feeling slightly somnolent, but roused by the knock on his noggin, he saw his beloved apple rolling across the floor of the church.

'I knew it was you!' he shouted, and filled with righteous indignation, rushed after the apple and picked it up. By now it was fit for neither man nor beast. In disgust he threw it back at the priest.

Now, as we know, gravity is quite a weak force. Mr Tomkin's arm, on the other hand, tempered by the toil of farm work, was a strong force. The throw was a good one and the apple hit Clerk on the forehead, sending him hard against the back of the pulpit from whence he proceeded to clatter down the stairs head-first until arriving at the feet of the still enraged Mr Tomkins.

He recovered quickly enough, especially as the rest of the congregation rushed to give him succour which, in his confused state, he misinterpreted as a lynch mob. As soon as he was fit enough he made some hasty concluding prayers and left, his stomach churning with embarrassment, not taking any part in the village festivities to celebrate their saint's day.

The people of Romsley had never seen anything like it. Inevitably the news travelled far and wide, and the numbers attending Mr Clerk's services actually went up as some previously very irregular churchgoers started coming along in the hopes that something similar might happen. Nothing did, which was a source of some annoyance to them.

A year went by and it was once again the time for the Romsley wake. The Reverend John Clerk took the service again, and was rather relieved that nothing untoward occurred during the course of it, although he was a little surprised to see many of the congregation leaving before him rather than waiting to shake his hand at the church door. As he came out of the darkness of the church into the light of day he was surprised to see a large crowd gathered in the churchyard, but was even more surprised when they started throwing apples at him. Now the people of Romsley prized themselves for their frugality. They were not going to use their precious cultivated apples for this purpose, but small crab apples that they found in the hedgerows. They also hurt Revd Clerk less, although you could not say the same about his dignity. This was considered such good sport that the tradition was kept up, year after year.

Even after Revd Clerk's time, the new incumbent was told that the custom of crabbing the parson was a custom that stretched back to time immemorial and he had to put up with it. However, by the middle of the nineteenth century, the Church of England was becoming unhappy with many of these old rural practices which, it was felt, encouraged begging, drunkenness and licentious behaviour. This was of course quite true, but provided the few opportunities that

the poor could indulge in the lifestyle of their betters. By this time the vicar of Romsley had noted that sticks and stones had started to appear amongst the crab apples, and decided that this was one custom that could very definitely be abolished. Old men shook their beards and warned that no good would come of it, and youths vented their spleen on the ducks on the village pond, but the practice fell into abeyance. Now anyone lobbing a crab apple at the vicar would be considered to be indulging in anti-social behaviour rather than following an old country custom.

TWENTY FOUR

THE FEMALE SOLDIER

Nowadays we do not think of a female soldier as an oxymoron, but in the eighteenth century, it was considered quite shocking that a member of the fair sex should dress in male attire and go off to kill her fellow men. It was the stuff of ballads and folk tales.

In the early part of that century there lived a hosier and dyer by the name of Samuel Snell. He and his wife Mary lived at No. 25 Friar Street, Worcester. They had six daughters, five of whom were quiet, domestic girls who liked nothing more than playing with their dolls or helping their mother with her chores. The sixth, Hannah, was a different thing altogether. She could not be got to stay home but was always playing with the boys in the street and getting into mischief. Her mother blamed Samuel, for telling all those stories about his father and brother who had gone as soldiers and performed many great deeds of valour until getting themselves killed.

But, when Hannah was seventeen, both her parents died and it was decided that the best thing for her was to send the girl to live with her married half-sister Susannah and her husband, James Grey, who lived in Wapping. For someone brought up in the small city of Worcester, the London Docks was an exciting place to be, full of strange sights and voices. Before long she fell under the spell of a handsome Dutch sailor by the name of James Summs. His blond hair, blue eyes and funny way of speaking made her forget about being a tomboy and discover her inner coquette. Summs was not displeased by the attentions of this pretty but strong willed young woman, and when Hannah became pregnant, he agreed to marry her. However, as the pregnancy progressed, he found domestic bliss not to his liking and headed off to the Docks and the first ship out of London.

Distraught, Hannah gave birth to a daughter, which she named after the only person who seemed to care about her; her sister Susannah. But the baby was sickly and died just a few months later. Grieving for her lost family, Hannah stole a suit of clothes belonging to her brother-in-law and set off in search of her love.

She had not gone far when she heard the stirring sound of a fife and drum coming down the street. She stopped to watch the soldiers pass and the sergeant at their head, a magnificent fellow with bright red coat, large yellow cuffs and a great deal of silver braid, saw the 'young man' watching and called a halt.

'And what's your name young fellow?'

'J…James Grey, sir.'

'Well, James Grey, you look like a man who would gladly fight for his king and country and destroy the murderous Scots.'

'I'm not sure I am sir.'

'Nonsense,' the sergeant pressed Hannah's bicep. 'That's an arm that can carry a musket. It looks as though Colonel Guise has another recruit.'

The next thing Hannah knew, she was being frogmarched along the road between two burly soldiers. She was taken to the barracks where she was given her own red coat, though one not as magnificent as the sergeant's, and made to practice drill with a heavy musket. Then she was informed that she was a private in the 6th Regiment of Foot, bound for the north to help 'Butcher' Cumberland pacify the rebellious Scots.

Every step on the road to Carlisle was a torment to her, not only because of the heavy pack she had to carry, but also because each of those steps took her further away from her beloved husband.

To make matters worse, the friendly recruiting sergeant was not nearly so pleasant to her now, but seemed to find fault with everything that she did. It got so bad that when they reached Carlisle, he ordered her to be flogged, which meant being stripped to the waist. This might have given the game away but luck was on Hannah's side. She had quite small breasts and, her arms being extended and fixed to the city gates and her face to the wall, she avoided detection. It did, however, convince her that army life was not for her. In Carlisle she was billeted with a family called Lucas in Little Park Street. It was easier than in camp for her to creep out at dead of night and get out of town before reveille.

She made her way to Portsmouth, begging and stealing her food as she went. It took her a month, but she had always been strong minded and was determined in her course. As soon as she came to the port she went to the marine barracks and asked to enlist. The officer was initially doubtful of this beardless youth, but when she proved she could handle a musket, she was welcomed to the ranks. She reasoned that going to sea would be the best way to find her sailor love.

Soon 'James Grey' sailed in the sloop Swallow, bound for India. Inevitably life on board put great strain on Hannah's ability to hide her true identity. Her delicacy, ability with a needle and the lack of hair on her chin earned her the nickname 'Molly Grey' before they had sailed through the Bay of Biscay. But her good nature, ability to hold her own in drinking contests and dexterity at musket drill had changed her name to 'Hearty Jemmy' by the time they reached India.

At every port they called at Hannah tried to get shore leave, visit every sailors' den she could find and then, when the moment was right, enquire about her friend James Summs and hope that someone had news of him, but she received no certain intelligence.

In India the East India Company was busy fighting the French, and any Indian who got in the way, trying to extend its empire. Every trained man was needed and Hannah found herself marching with pack and musket towards some uncertain future. Not wishing to betray her sex she fought bravely and took part in two battles, those of Pondicherry and Devicotta. She was wounded eleven times in the legs and once in the groin. Naturally it was the later that was likely to prove most troublesome, but she was able to hide the wound until she could find some quiet place where she could dig the musket ball out with her hands. She was saved by the low velocity of muskets and the care of a young Indian girl who had taken a liking to this strange young Englishman. For two days she lay in a fever, her life in the balance, but her strong Worcester constitution saw her through.

It was while she was recovering from her wounds that she at last received some news concerning James Summs, but it was not good news; he had been hanged for murder in Genoa. The whole point of her existence had been taken from her. It was therefore with relief that she heard that her regiment had been ordered back to England. She still played the part of Hearty Jemmy until her ship docked in London. When she was safely ensconced in a tavern with some of her shipmates, she told them that she was leaving the marines. They laughed and asked James Grey how he proposed to do that.

'Why gentlemen, James Grey will cast off his skin like a snake and become a new creature. In a word, gentlemen, I am as much a woman as my mother was, and my real name is Hannah Snell.'

With that she unfastened her shirt just enough to prove she was telling the truth. Naturally there was consternation among her friends but, when the hubbub had died down and it was agreed that she no longer qualified to be a marine, her companions tried to persuade her that since she had completed five years' service, her best course of action was to seek a pension for her service.

She was at first reluctant, but eventually gave way and drew up a petition setting out her position and presented it to the Duke of Cumberland himself while he was reviewing troops at Horse Guards. He was naturally as shocked as her shipmates had been, but agreed that the matter should be looked into. Of course, the news got out and Hannah became the toast of the town; pamphlets were written about her and she was asked to make guest appearances at many London theatres, her arrival and her singing humorous and entertaining songs and the recounting of her exploits being greeted with thunderous applause.

Eventually the Army, although it would do anything to avoid paying a bill, agreed that her statement could be proved true and she was honourably discharged and awarded a small pension. With the money she was able to buy a pub in Wapping, which she called The Female Soldier. However it was not a success, and she moved to Newbury where she was to marry twice more.

In 1785 she moved to Stoke Newington, to stay with her son from her second marriage. However, in 1791 she had to be taken to the Bethlehem Hospital, the dreaded Bedlam, suffering from what was described by a newspaper as 'the most deplorable infirmity that can afflict human nature', probably some form of dementia.

She died six months later and was buried where she wanted to be, in a plot reserved for old soldiers in Chelsea Hospital. As one of the songs she used to sing on the London stage reminds us:

All ye noble British spirits
That midst dangers glory sought,
Let it lessen not your merit,
That a woman bravely fought.
Cupid slyly first enrolled me,
Pallas next her force did bring,
Pressed my heart to venture boldly
For my love and for my King.

TWENTY~FIVE

THE DEVIL AND
THE FARMER

The people of Worcestershire are noted for being pious and God-fearing. So the poor old Devil had a hard time of it. Once he was reduced to such misery that he had to ask a farmer down Comberton way for a job.

'I don't take just anyone on,' said the farmer. 'What can you do?'

'I can do anything,' said the Devil, who was not noted for his modesty.

'I've heard that before,' said the farmer. 'Anyway, I've got to thresh this stack of wheat. Help me with that and I'll see how you get on.'

So they set to work. The Devil was as good as his word. While the farmer got on top of the stack and threw down the sheaves, the Devil set about threshing them. But he only needed one stroke of the flail to knock all the corn out of a sheaf, and then he was ready for the next one. He poor old farmer could not keep up. He was soon sweating with the exertion.

'Hold on a minute,' he said. 'Time to change places. You come up here and throw the sheaves down to me.'

'As you like,' said the Devil.

The farmer carefully climbed down the ladder, but as he was coming down, the Devil just sprung up from the floor onto the top of the stack. The farmer looked at him suspiciously. There was something odd about this fellow.

'Ready?' called the Devil, but before the farmer could say anything, the Devil stuck his pitchfork into ten sheaves at once and threw them down onto the threshing floor.

That'll do for a bit,' said the farmer, and he set about threshing what was there while the Devil sat down on the sheaves and waited. When the farmer had finished the Devil threw another ten down and the farmer threshed away. So it went on, until before nightfall, they had finished the whole thing, something the farmer had expected to take a couple of days.

So he was quite satisfied with his new man and agreed to take him on. But he could not help thinking hard about him that evening. There was definitely something odd about him. He dressed as any working man dressed, apart from really big boots. But, if the man had some deformity of his feet, it certainly did not stop him working hard.

Lying in bed at night, he could not drop off to sleep thinking about the mystery. In the end all his tossing and turning woke up his wife.

'For goodness sake, what's the matter with you?'

'I'm thinking about the new labourer I've taken on. He's a good worker but there's certainly something wrong about him.'

'Well, instead of keeping me awake all night, why don't you go and see old Bill Banton in the morning. He'll put you straight.'

The farmer could see the sense in this. Old Bill was regarded as the font of all wisdom thereabouts. He always gave good advice. That put the farmer's mind at rest and he was soon off to sleep and snoring like a good 'un.

The next morning he went off to see Bill Banton and told him about his worries. Bill had a think about it, puffing on his pipe, and then said, 'Well, it's as plain to me as your face. Your new man is the Devil hisself.'

A chill went down the farmer's spine. 'The Devil! Then how am I going to get rid of him?' Although the man had been no trouble so far, no one wants the Devil as a co-worker. Who knows how it might end up?

'Now then, that's not so easy.' Bill took a long draw on his pipe and the farmer did not know if he could not think of anything or he was just doing it for effect. Eventually Bill put his pipe down and looked at him very seriously. 'In my way of looking at it, the only way you can get rid of him now you've taken him on is by giving him a job he can't do. The Devil doesn't like to be bested in anything; he'll be so annoyed, he'll up and leave.'

The farmer walked home, thinking about things. As soon as he turned into the yard there was the Devil sitting on the mounting block, waiting for him.

'So master, what's to be done this morning?'

Now that he knew who he was, the farmer was quite terrified speaking to him, but he tried to hide it. He had also been thinking of what task to set the Devil all the way home and he thought he had got it. 'Right, I want you to go into the barn and count the number of grains that we threshed out yesterday.'

The Devil did not look a bit abashed, but went straight to the barn. In a few minutes he was back.

'855,876.' he said.

The farmer's jaw dropped. 'You sure you haven't missed any?'

'No, I've counted every one.'

Now the farmer realised that he had absolutely no way of knowing if the Devil was right or not, because he himself had no way of knowing how many grains of wheat there were.

'Well, that sounds about right,' said the farmer, trying to hide his confusion. 'Not a bad harvest.' He thought quickly. 'Right, the missus'll need some water for cooking. Go down to the stream with this barrel and get some, will you, and you can take this sieve to help you.'

So the Devil went off and the farmer chuckled to himself, thinking he had seen the last of that fellow. But within a few minutes the Devil was back, with a full barrel of water. 'What next?' he said.

That is how it went on through the day, with the farmer trying to think up all kinds of impossible tasks and the Devil doing them before the farmer could think of the next one. By the end of it he was almost driven to distraction.

'Why are you in such a funny mood?' asked his wife. 'You're ahead of your work aren't you?'

The farmer did not want to tell her the truth in case it worried her, so he just said he was tired and tried to eat some supper although, in truth, he was not terribly hungry.

He went to sit in his chair by the fire, feeling a bit gloomy. Then he remembered that the top field needed a mow. That gave him an idea. He jumped up off the chair, much to his wife's shock, and dashed into his workshop, where he collected a load of old harrow tines he had saved because they might come in useful one day. By now it was nearly dark, but still he went up to the top field and started driving the spikes into the ground, although he was careful only to do that on one side of the field.

When the Devil turned up for work the next day, the farmer was waiting for him with two scythes. 'This morning I want to mow the top field. You up for helping me?'

'All right,' said the Devil.

When they got to the field the farmer said, 'You take this side of the field, and I'll take the other.' Off course you can guess in which side of the field the spikes were hidden. They set to work, but the farmer kept an eye on the Devil, expecting him to have to keep stopping to sharpen his scythe, and to get discouraged. But he saw that the Devil was cutting through the spikes almost as if they were not there. After a while he saw the farmer looking at him.

'You've got some terrible burdocks in this field, master.'

It was the farmer who threw down his scythe in disgust. 'Tell you what,' he said. 'You're doing so well here. Why don't you carry on alone and I'll get on with something else?'

The Devil not objecting, the farmer went back to the farmhouse. He sat down in the porch with his head in his hands, thinking he was never going to be free of him.

Lucky for him, an old gypsy woman happened at that moment to come up to the house to try to sell her wares. 'World not treating you right?' she said. Like any good salesperson she could size up the situation immediately. Because he needed someone to talk to, the farmer told her the problem. The old gypsy sucked her teeth. 'Well, that's a corker.'

'Try telling me something I don't know.'

'You're going about things the wrong way. When your man comes back, give him some of your wife's curly tresses and tell him to go and hammer them straight. See how he likes that.'

The farmer was so grateful he gave her more coins than she had been expecting all day, and she went away quite happy. The farmer went into the house and explained to his wife that he had taken on the Devil and now needed some of her hair so he could get rid of him. When she stopped screaming, he managed to get her to cut off some of her curly tresses, and the farmer went outside to wait.

Before too long the Devil came sauntering down the path. 'I've finished the mowing, master. What else would you like me to do?'

The farmer produced the hair. 'My wife's off to market tomorrow. The fashions changed and all the other wives now have straight hair. She can't face being seen with hers curly. Be a good chap and pop into the workshop and beat this straight.' So the Devil did. For a while the farmer listened to the hammer going nineteen to the dozen. After a while, some very strong language mixed with the hammering. Then the language predominated over the hammering. Suddenly there was a flash of blue light and then silence. When the farmer checked the workshop it was empty, apart from a very strong smell of sulphur. And, as much as the farmer always kept checking over his shoulder, the Devil was never seen there again.

TWENTY SIX

THE SEVEN WHISTLERS

Belief in the seven whistlers was described by John Cotton, writing in the Bromsgrove Messenger in 1909, as an old Worcestershire delusion. In fact it was not just in Worcestershire, but also all along the Welsh border that these were feared. They were birds, or some say the souls of the dead, that cried out in the night, prophesying disaster. To wake up in the dark and hear their cries was to know that some terrible doom was liable to overtake you or someone that you loved.

Some said that you would only hear six and that would be bad enough, but those six were forever searching for the seventh, and if they ever found it, the world would end. Birds were generally believed to be able to act as messengers between the worlds. Horace Walpole tells the story of an old lady in Worcester who kept a number of caged birds in her pew in the cathedral in the belief that her dead daughter would communicate with her through them. The Dean tolerated this because she also happened to be a considerable benefactress to the cathedral.

Though this might be the belief of the peasantry and the easily suggestible, by the eighteenth century, educated men of the Enlightenment would have laughed at the idea. Such a man was Tom, the second Lord Lyttleton of Hagley Hall.

His father, Sir George Lyttleton, Bt, had been a very ambitious man. He tore down his ancestral – but Elizabethan – mansion and rebuilt Hagley Hall in the latest style. He was a skilled politician who saw his best chance as opposing the prime minister, Robert Walpole, and after Walpole's fall, was rewarded with being appointed Chancellor of the Exchequer. Not being content with being a mere baronet, he was raised to the peerage as Lord Lyttleton.

If he was ambitious for himself, he was even more ambitious for his son, Tom. He decided that he was a boy with amazing gifts, who when he grew up, would make the Lyttleton name known far and wide. He did not know how right he was going to be but for all the wrong reasons.

Lord Lyttleton's terrible error was to send his son on the Grand Tour. Most sons of the rich were sent to Europe with the hope that some of its high culture would rub off on them. Whatever kind of boy he had been before, on his travels young Tom discovered wine, women and the gaming tables. He enjoyed himself immensely.

On his return to England, he had no intention of settling down to country life in quiet old Worcestershire. He much preferred the clubs and theatres of London. His father found him a nice Parliamentary seat in Bewdley, hoping that the excitement of politics would turn the young man's head away from depravity. Tragically the beaten candidate complained, and on appeal, the election was found to be corrupt even by eighteenth-century standards. The result was overturned. Tom now had no distractions to keep him from the life of a rake.

Naturally Lord Lyttleton bitterly reproached his son for taking to a life of dissipation and destroying his early promise, especially as he, himself, was considered a very upright member of society. There was a distinct cooling between the two and Tom took to spending most of his time in London or, when creditors became too pressing, in Paris.

Tom did one thing to please his father; he married a rich young widow, Apphia Witt, even if a little too soon after her husband's death for decorum's sake. But, if the old man had thought married life would tame his son, he was sadly disappointed. Within a few months Tom was back at the gaming tables of London, leaving his unfortunate wife at Hagley and having little more to do with her. They were never to have any children. The only woman he seemed to care for was one of his dissolute companions, Alicia Dawson, and Lord Lyttleton had no intention of letting that sort of woman over the threshold of Hagley Hall.

It was in Paris that Tom heard the news that his father had died and he was now the 2nd Lord Lyttleton. He rushed back to Hagley to sort out the funeral arrangements and to find that his respectable father had left debts of over £26,000; a huge amount then, incurred by building and trying to maintain the new Hagley Hall. In the future, if any of his relations reproved him for his gambling he would tell them he was forced to continue it to pay his father's debts.

Over the next six years Tom earned the name of 'the wicked Lord Lyttleton', not only for the way he had treated his wife, but also for other acts of debauchery, most notably seducing all three of the Miss Ampletts. To be fair to him, he was a conscientious member of the House of Lords, speaking in favour of negotiation with the American colonies rather than war and conciliation over the worsening tensions in Ireland.

Although only thirty-seven, his dissolute lifestyle was beginning to catch up with him. He started to suffer from fits in which he felt he was suffocating, but this did not stop him carrying on drinking and gambling. One night in November he was asleep at his London residence, Hill House in Berkeley Square, when he had a terrible dream. He dreamt that a white bird, like a dove, flew into his room and then transformed into a woman, clothed in a shroud, who told him his time on this earth was almost over and he must prepare himself for death.

'I hope not soon,' said Lord Lyttleton.

'Yes, within three days,' replied the woman and then vanished.

Understandably agitated, he rung for his valet and told him about the premonition, but eventually settled down to the idea that it was merely a dream. At breakfast the next morning he recounted his story to his guests, and seemed more subdued than normal. But they assured him that it was mere fancy and eventually he regained his normal humour. Of those who saw him over the next few days, some reported him depressed while others thought him unchanged, though still suffering from his fits of breathlessness.

At breakfast on 27 November he remarked, 'If I live out tonight I shall have jockeyed the ghost, for this is the third day.'

He was due to travel to another of his houses, Pitt Place near Epsom, that morning with his guests. On their arrival, and without his knowledge, all the clocks in the house and all the watches of the guests were advanced half an hour by way of a friendly trick.

That evening Lord Lyttleton played cards with his friends with his accustomed charm and gaiety. At half-past eleven he retired to his bedroom and got ready for bed, taking a dose of rhubarb and mint water. His valet recalled that he was constantly looking at his pocket watch throughout this process. After he got into bed, he asked to look at his valet's watch and was pleased to see that wanted only two minutes before midnight.

At a quarter past twelve he put his watch to his ear to make sure it was still working and said, 'This mysterious lady is not a true prophetess I find. Come, I'll wait no longer, get me my medicine; I'll take it and try to sleep.'

Then he saw that the valet was stirring the medicine with a toothpick, scolded him for it and told him to go and find a teaspoon.

When the valet returned he found Lord Lyttleton in a fit, his chin forced down against his chest owing to the elevation of the pillows. Instead of rushing to his aid, the fellow panicked and went to raise the alarm. By the time he and his alarmed guests came back to the room, Lord Lyttleton was dead.

Miles Andrews was a close friend of Tom's but had been forced to leave the party at Pitt Place because he had pressing business in Dartford. That night he was asleep in bed at his business partner's house when the curtains were suddenly thrown back and there was Lord Lyttleton, in his nightgown and nightcap, staring at him.

Andrews let out a vile oath, thinking his friend was playing a stupid trick on him. He struggled to light his bedside candle but, when he turned back, the figure had disappeared. He called his valet and demanded where the devil Lord Lyttleton was hiding, but the valet just looked at him blankly and said he had not seen his lordship since that morning when they had left Pitt Place.

Now the whole household was aroused and the building searched, but no trace of Lord Lyttleton was found.

Andrews was convinced that, somehow, Tom had played a prank on him until that afternoon, when the news of Tom's death reached him.

Lord Lyttleton's premonition and his subsequent death became the talk of both London and Worcestershire society. Various rational explanations were put forward. Had Lyttleton poisoned himself and put out the story of the ghost as a smokescreen? But that did not explain why he had not taken the poison earlier, not after, as he thought, the time of the ghost's warning. Was the 'ghost' one of the many wronged women in his lordship's life who had succeeded in scaring him to death? If so, she was remarkably clever in not being seen by anyone else in Berkeley Square. Whatever the truth of it, Lord Lyttleton's is a story still told, to show that even the greatest of us cannot escape the call of death when it comes.

TWENTY SEVEN

JACK AND THE FARMER'S WIFE

For once the wars were over, which ought to have been a good thing, but it put Jack out of work as a soldier and he had to go on the tramp, looking for work at the farms that he passed. He found good pickings in Worcestershire, because the inhabitants were impressed by the splendour of his uniform. Once he was even mistaken for an angel over Bewdley way.

It happened like this. He knocked on the door of a farmhouse one day, and it was answered by an elderly farmer's wife who thought this must be a very important person to be dressed so, and quickly invited him in.

'Where are you from?' she asked him.

'From Paris,' replied Jack. The old woman misheard and thought he said, 'From Paradise.'

'Then you must know my poor late husband, John Jones.'

Jack was quick on the uptake and realised there had been a mistake and he might have an advantage by it. Jack said he might and, as the woman filled in some details about him to jog Jack's memory, it was found that Jack did indeed know the fellow well. He assured her that John Jones was very comfortable in heaven, only tired of having nothing to do, and was asking people for money so he could set up a pepper mill.

'Ah,' said the old woman, 'That is so like my dear John. He was always looking for ways of making money. Hang on a minute.'

With that she went over to the chimney corner and came back with an old stocking. 'Here's ten guineas he saved, but died before he could spend it. Take this and the old grey mare you see outside. That'll help turn the pepper mill.'

Jack thanked her profusely and promised, when next he bumped into John Jones, he would hand over the money and the horse. Then he was out of there as fast as the horse could gallop.

When the woman's son returned from the fields and heard her story, he could not believe that he could be related to someone so stupid. He set out in pursuit and soon came upon a shepherd; he asked the fellow if he had seen a soldier on a grey mare.

'That I have,' said the shepherd. 'I saw 'em just now. They were flying through the air up above that field. I've never seen anything like it.'

The young man returned to his home shaking his head and wondering if perhaps his mother had been right all along. The shepherd took out a nice shiny guinea from his pocket and kissed it, because Jack was always generous and liked to share his good fortune.

But money is soon spent and horses soon sold, so old Jack was back on the tramp again. One evening he came to a farm near Suckley and decided to try his luck. He walked up to the door as bold as any old soldier and knocked. It was opened by a young farmer's wife who looked at him suspiciously.

'Good evening your highness,' said Jack, 'Have you any odd jobs you need doing about the place in return for a bed for the night and a bite to eat?'

'Get out of here you good for nothing. We're poor folk here and haven't got food to throw away on beggars like you. I've hardly got enough food to feed my husband and myself, let alone any idiot that comes off the road.' With that she slammed the door shut in Jack's face.

Now Jack knew better than to negotiate in this sort of situation. He was just about to walk out of the farmyard and try his luck elsewhere when he noticed an old barn near the farmhouse. It was full of nice comfortable hay, the night was coming on and there was rain in the air, so Jack reasoned that the young woman's outburst did not apply to the barn. Glancing back to make sure that she was not watching him from the window, he slipped through the open door and looked around. He decided to climb up to hay loft, and made himself a fine bed by the opening where the hay was tossed in. He made himself comfortable, reasoning that, although he had an empty belly, at least he had a warm and dry place to spend the night, so he could count himself pretty lucky.

He was just falling asleep when he heard footsteps coming through the farmyard. He looked out of the opening and saw it was a young curate hurrying along in the rain that had now come on quite heavily.

Thinking to have some amusement at the curate's expense, Jack propped himself on his elbow ready to watch what would happen when he knocked on the door, expecting he would get as warm a response as he had done.

The curate knocked lightly on the door and it was opened. However, Jack was surprised to see him invited straight in.

Through the window of the house he saw the housewife throw her arms around the curate and give him a big kiss. 'I had no idea religion was so popular in these parts,' thought Jack.

The curate was sat down at the kitchen table and the farmer's wife produced a fine apple pie and a jug of cider. He was just about to tuck into this fine feast when the clip clop of horse's hooves could be heard entering the yard.

Jack saw the old farmer sitting hunched in the saddle against the rain, looking as if he was carrying the weight of the world on his shoulders. The farmer's wife also looked out and saw who it was. Now there was panic in the kitchen. The apple pie was hidden in the oven, the cider jug up in the rafters behind a beam, and even the poor curate was persuaded to climb into an empty cider hogshead barrel that could accommodate him well enough.

While all this was going on, the old farmer tied up his horse in the stable and made the old creature comfortable for the night. Then he walked into the house. The greeting between husband and wife seemed pretty perfunctory to Jack's eyes, but he was not an expert on the matter so made no judgement about it.

The farmer sat down at the table, and the wife ladled out some thin gruel from a pot on the stove and placed it before her husband. Even at that distance, and with nothing in his belly, it did not look too appetising to Jack.

A piece of hay scratched Jack's neck and, as he watched the farmer glumly eating his poor meal, he thought he might do something about it. He jumped down from the hay loft and out into the yard and knocked again on the farmhouse door.

It was the farmer who opened it this time, not looking too pleased to be interrupted from his supper, poor as it was.

'Have you any odd jobs for an ex-soldier about the place that need doing in return for a bite to eat and a bed for the night?' asked Jack.

The farmer thought for a while, clearly a bit slow on the uptake. 'I don't see as I have, but I won't put a man out on a night like this. You're welcome to share what supper we have and settle down in front of the fire.'

So Jack came in and settled his feet under the table, despite the dark looks the farmer's wife gave him. A bowl of the gruel was set before him, though the woman managed to splash a good part of it over Jack as she set it down.

Jack and the farmer finished their meal and leaned back, each contemplating their still empty bellies.

'That was a good meal,' said Jack.

'I wish I could offer you a better one,' replied the farmer.

'You know, what we could do with now to finish it off would be a good apple pie, made with good Worcester apples.'

The farmer laughed. 'It's a long while since I tasted one of those, myself.'

'You know,' said Jack, 'being a soldier you get to discover all kinds of useful skills, and I think I've picked up more than my fair share on my travels.'

'Like what?' asked the farmer.

'If I told you I could make an apple pie appear in this room, would you believe me?'

'I would not.'

Jack closed his eyes and put his fingers to his temples. 'Apple pie, apple pie, straightway come to my eye. Abracadabra!' Then he pointed at the oven. 'You go and check in there.'

The farmer did so and was astonished to find the pie there. He brought it out and called his wife. 'Look what this traveller has found for us.' His wife turned a deep red but did not say anything. The farmer insisted that all three of them sit down at the table and tuck in, which they did in silence, on Jack's part because he was enjoying himself.

When he had finished Jack pushed his plate away from him and leaned back in his chair. 'You know, what would wash that down well would be a good glass of Worcestershire cider.'

The farmer laughed and pointed at the hogshead. 'That thing is as empty as heaven. You'll have to wait a few months for the next crop of apples.'

Again Jack closed his eyes and put his fingers to his forehead. 'Jug of cider, jug of cider, come to me, don't be a hider. Abracadabra!' He pointed up at the cross beam and the farmer looked up and discovered the jug hidden there.

'You're a marvel!' said the farmer, but the farmer's wife just gave him a very funny look.

The two men sat at their ease, drinking the cider. When it was finished Jack put his glass on the table and said, 'Although I'm an old soldier, I've remained a religious man. What we could do with now is a blessing from a parson.'

The farmer laughed. 'This is an isolated spot. The old vicar, nor even his young curate, never comes up here.'

'Nevertheless,' said Jack, and he closed his eyes and put his fingers to his forehead. 'Man of God, man of God, don't be a sly and secret sod. Abracadabra!' He pointed at the hogshead, and even the farmer was not too surprised when he lifted up the lid and discovered the curate inside.

After a hasty blessing, the curate went on his way and Jack settled down to a comfortable night in front of the fire. In the morning he got a good breakfast and a gold sovereign from the farmer for such an evening that he had never had in a long time.

As he was going down the lane away from the farm, he saw the farmer's wife standing at the corner. 'I'm in for a good cussing.' Jack thought to himself.

But instead, as Jack drew near, the farmer's wife held out another gold sovereign. 'That's for not telling,' she said, and so Jack went on his way with a full belly, a smile on his lips and a small fortune in his pocket. But what he did with it is another story.

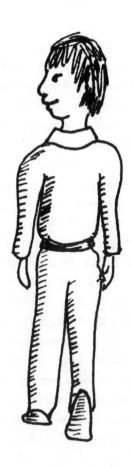

TWENTY EIGHT

TWOPENNY PRISS

According to Katherine Briggs, this story was collected by the folklorist Ruth Tongue in the 1940s from her grandmother in Worcestershire, who remembered hearing it in about 1878.

Daughters are difficult things. They never grow up as you expect them to. Old Mrs Thomas always swore she did her best, but her daughter Marjorie grew up all hoity-toity like, with a way of sneering at everything. Poor Mrs Thomas knew she would never find a husband.

Marjorie did not care about that until she started looking for one, and discovering that it was indeed the case. Eventually she found a small shopkeeper who was more anxious to have someone who would work for free in the shop than companionship in the kitchen, though he came to regret his decision.

She had a daughter, and as is the way of such things, she brought her up to be as high and mighty as herself, or even more so.

Eventually the poor old shopkeeper caught a chill and was happy enough to die off out of it. But Marjorie had got a taste for married life now, although it was not the married life you or I would have cared for. More like having your very own punching bag.

But she set her sights on a well-to-do farmer over Peopleton way. He, being a bachelor and not knowing about the wiles of women, was happy and flattered to go along with it, until she married him.

She led him a right old dance, and her daughter was no better. They had gone up in the world, and were sure to let the whole world know that it was still several degrees below what it should be. If the farmer let them down by slurping his tea or not holding his knife correctly, they would certainly let him know it. And they would let him know it, even if there was company present. For all their new frills and finery, they screamed and gabbled like geese.

The farmer grew sad and tired and ashamed. The only course of action seemed a change of neighbourhood. When he was not avoiding the beaks of his womenfolk, the farmer was an open and honest soul, so he talked over his thoughts with his men. 'I'm thinking of taking Bullitt Farm.'

''Tis a good farm, master,' they all agreed.

'So I hear.'

'But it has a queer name for itself indoors,' they said.

'We won't be much indoors.'

'The Miss and Missus will.'

'That'll be their lookout then. If there's anything there I would think they will be a match for it.'

So to Bullitt Farm they all went. The farmer worked outside every hour of daylight, and a few over, and his wife and her daughter lazed about inside. So it might have gone on for some time, but there was one room in the house that was nailed up. Of course the women insisted that it must be unnailed and they turned it into their grand parlour, just like her ladyship's at the great hall.

Yet it could not be got quite right for them. There was another door in the room that was locked, and the previous tenants had not left the key. Of course they said it must be broken down immediately, but the farmer said the men were too busy on the farm to see to it at present. That caused a scene.

These two grand ladies could not be expected to do any work around the house, so a girl was fetched from the workhouse. She was called Twopenny Priss, because that was all the overseer said she was worth. The women were happy to give her the nickname and to use it constantly although the farmer never did. He could see that she was a kindly girl, though big-boned, and it made him feel sad to see the way that she was treated; although he could think of no way of mending it, short of putting her back on the road.

One day Miss was reading in the parlour. The door that was locked creaked and swung open a little.

'Come in, whoever you are and be dratted,' said the girl in a petulant tone, annoyed at being interrupted. So in IT came.

What IT was exactly I cannot tell you, because I did not see it, and so still have my wits about me. Have you ever woken in the dark of the night in a cold sweat and darker foreboding and been thankful that you cannot fully remember the dream you have just had? That was IT.

It was the cold mist that came with IT that made her look up. She gave such a scream that all the hens ran squawking up to the barn rafters for safety. It took no notice. IT just tossed her out of the open window, head-down into the newly turned flower beds.

When they dug her out, she started running and she did not stop until she met a gypsy. He, looking at all her furbelows, thought he was onto a good thing, and got her to run away with him.

Whether she mended her manners I do not know, but I do know the gypsy had a good blackthorn stick which he kept handy.

After this, the mother could not be comforted, having lost her partner in misery. She drove everyone crazy with her temper and the only thing that could be done with her was to sit her down in the parlour.

The door creaked and swung open a little.

'Drat, you fool! Come on in and hurry up about it.' So in IT came.

She gave a yell that frightened the pig into a fit and she ran out of the room, with IT after her.

She ran up to the attic, screaming all the time, but IT caught up with her and tossed her out of the attic window, and she broke her neck.

They gave her a decent funeral and it was not long before the farmer got back his kindly old ways and the men folk whistled about their work and Twopenny Priss sang as she cooked and scrubbed and polished and swept. When we go, we leave something behind, and we would be wise to make that a good thing rather than have people glad to see the back of us.

After a while, being of a kindly nature, she felt sorry that the parlour was just gathering dust.

The farm men warned her.

'There's something up there, an unquiet spirit. It's best to leave it alone.'

'The poor lonely thing,' said Twopenny Priss. 'And not a Christian soul to help it.'

'Remember what happened to Miss and Missus.'

'I'll take my Bible and say my prayers, for me and for IT,' she said.

No matter whatever else they said to her, she went off with her broom and Bible and set to clean the parlour. In a little while the door creaked and swung open.

'Come in and welcome, in God's name,' said Twopenny Priss. So in IT came.

The mist was bitter cold, but Twopenny Priss took out her little Bible and held it out in front of her.

'In the name of the Lord, why do you trouble me?'

The mist started to dissolve, and instead there stood the ghost of the old miser who had lived in the house many centuries before. He had died alone and unloved, and mystery had always surrounded what he had done with all his money.

The ghost beckoned her to follow him into the small room. 'Come!' he said. She did so.

In the room there was a hearth. The figure stood by it and pointed down at the hearth stone.

'So that's where you hid your gold? You poor unhappy thing; it weighs too heavy for you to get away, and you can't take it with you.'

The ghost said, 'Lift!' and Twopenny Priss did so; she was a good, strong girl. In the hole there was a small chest, and in the chest, bags of gold coins.

Then the ghost lifted up its arms and cried with a loud voice, 'Free at last!', and then he disappeared for ever.

Being an honest girl, Twopenny Priss took the chest to the farmer. When he saw all the gold he said, 'Why, here is a fine dowry for you.'

'But who'd marry me, even with all this gold? I'm too homely for a husband.'

Tears came to the farmer's eyes. 'Bless your kind, loving heart. I would, and I would tomorrow.'

So he did. Now, to say they all lived happily ever after would not be true. After all, they were real people, not characters in a fairy story. But they came close.

TWENTY NINE

THE WHITE WITCH
OF KIDDERMINSTER

In the old days, before the welfare state, every town and village had one or two women whose job was to keep society functioning. They would help bring babies into the world, deal with all the aches and pains that life, especially a hard labouring life, is prone to, and then, when their best efforts failed, help lay out the corpse for burial. Like the middle-class doctors who despised them, they generally inherited their knowledge and skills from a parent. In their case, often a mother or grandmother would teach them the use of herbs, and possibly a few potions and charms as well.

Such a woman was Becky Swan, who lived in a dirty and dilapidated cottage on what is now Station Hill in Kidderminster in the middle of the nineteenth century. Her appearance certainly inspired confidence that she was up to the job, her hair being a mass of elf locks, and her face having a thin and haggard appearance and an eagle-like beak for a nose. While most of her profession contented themselves in curing the body, she went further and specialised in seeing into the future and finding lost property. In this she was aided by three large cats named the Queen of Sheba, Queen Caroline and Princess Charlotte.

During a consultation with a client, the cats would often be present, intently listening to proceedings. Often one would jump onto Becky's shoulder and purr loudly into her ear, upon which Becky would explain what the cat had said. She also claimed to possess four magic dogs, Liverpool (after a feared Prime Minister), Victoria, Pretty and St John, although these were not so often in evidence. One local wag claimed to have climbed into Becky's cottage one night and stolen St John but the case was never proved.

The inside of the cottage was dark and mysterious; stuffed bats and owls hung from the rafters, and snake skins and dusty bottles covered the shelves and tables.

Certainly Becky had the uncanny ability to find lost property. Once, a family approached her over the loss of their donkey. After discussing the matter with her cats Becky told them not to worry, Neddy would soon be returned to them. Sure enough, the following afternoon, a gypsy knocked on their door, with the missing donkey on a rein. He said that he had found it wandering on Hartlebury Common, and on enquiring, as any honest fellow would, as to whom had lost a donkey, was directed to them. The family were so glad to get the donkey back that both gypsy and Becky were well rewarded. Of course there were some that said Becky and the gipsies were in league together, but they did not say it very loudly. Though certainly, when Becky herself lost twelve half crowns and a gold ring, the cats were singularly unhelpful to her in getting them back.

Then Becky fell foul of the authorities. A servant girl came to her wanting to know who her true love might be, there being several candidates. Becky told her, for a fee. When the girl's mistress heard about this, she was outraged and complained to the magistrates, and Becky was had up on a charge of obtaining money by false pretences. The magistrate had never heard anything so outrageous – that people could take such advantage of simple young women – and found her guilty, and sentenced her to thirty days in gaol.

Becky regarded the magistrate with what might loosely be described as an evil look. 'Why should I be worried about you?' she said. 'You'll be dead before I get out of clink.'

The magistrate, who had never felt in better health, laughed at her, and of course, all the court officials did as well. Yet, just three days before Becky was due to be released, the magistrate had an apoplectic fit on the bench and was dead before he could be carried home. Her reputation rose immensely. She hung a sign outside her hovel:

> Rebecca Swan, town and country letter writer to all parts, giving advice on all periods. No need to apply without recommendation. I have been wrongfully used. Wishes to do justice, love mercy and walk humbly with God.

When Thomas Slaughter was arrested for the capital crime of rick-burning he protested his innocence, but when he heard that a man had been sent to Becky Swan to find out the truth he changed his plea, 'as someone was off to Bec Swan of Kidderminster and she was sure to know.' He was duly hanged; the only man in Worcestershire executed as part of the Agrarian Unrest of the nineteenth century.

Shamans have always used some powerful drug to put them in touch with the spirit world. Our ancestors made great use of magic mushrooms; the people of the Amazon have a fondness for ayahuasca. Becky used gin, which she consumed in prodigious quantities. The efficacy of it could be heard by her neighbours late at night, as she crashed about and shouted and swore at the spirits. In the morning, her face covered in scratches and bruises, she would tell them she had received her wounds fighting off all manner of witches and devils.

Those who used her services but felt a little guilty, consoled themselves with the fact that she was a white witch and had never done anything evil. That belief was severely tested in November 1850. A huge black cat was seen in the neighbourhood that the local dogs would have nothing to do with. It was seen to walk up the path to Becky Swan's cottage and tap on the door. When Becky opened it and saw the cat, her face went

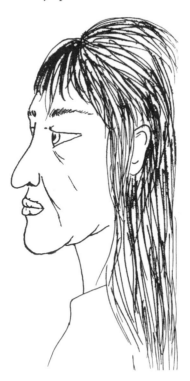

ashen and she let out a cry of horror. The cat calmly walked past her into the cottage and Becky closed the door.

After three days it was realised that Becky had not been seen in her usual haunts. A nervous crowd gathered outside her home, trying to decide what to do. The neighbours recollected that they had heard screams coming from the cottage a few nights ago but thought it was just old Becky communicating with the spirits in the usual fashion.

Eventually a few of the braver souls decided to break down the door to see what was up. When they did so, the first thing they saw was the huge cat sitting on the hearth rug. It took one long look at them, which they would not forget in a hurry, and then dashed up the chimney and was never seen again. As for Becky, all they could find was a pile of ashes in front of the cold fire, with just her legs sticking out of it.

There were many that said that the devil had come to claim his own. Others thought that poor old Becky had been so completely sozzled with gin that she had tumbled into the fire and been too drunk to get out. The ashes were gathered together and buried, but the local vicar refused to have them put in consecrated ground. Where they were put was a closely guarded secret, but I would advise anyone digging in the Kidderminster area who comes across an old pot to leave well alone, and let it stay where it is.

THIRTY

WHO PUT BELLA IN THE WYCH ELM?

Bird-nesting, the taking of wild birds' eggs from their nests, is today considered a reprehensible crime and you can quite rightly be put in gaol for it. However, in the 1940s it was considered a right and proper occupation for a young lad. So, one fine April day in 1943, four such young lads, Bob Farmer, Bob Hart, Fred Payne and Tom Willetts, decided to try their luck in Hagley Woods. This was part of the Hagley Estate, owned by Lord Cobham, so they would be trespassing, but this only made the enterprise more exciting.

Not having much success, eventually they came to an old hollow tree known locally as a wych elm although, if they had been serious naturalists, they would have spotted it as a wych hazel. The oldest and most venturesome of the boys, Bob Farmer, volunteered to climb up the tree, to a nest he could see in one of the top-most branches. As he climbed up he naturally glanced down into the hollow trunk.

'Hey, there's something there,' he called down to his companions.

'What is it?' asked Fred.

'It looks like an animal's skull.'

This caused great excitement amongst the boys. Eggs were fine as far as they went, but a skull would be a great addition to their collection.

Bob shinned back down the tree until he could reach it. He leant down, tugged and pulled the object up. When he could see it clearly he almost let it go, and it was only because his three friends were below that he stopped himself from screaming. 'It's h … human.'

'What?'

'It's a human skull. Take a look if you don't believe me.' Anxious to be rid of it, he threw the thing away from him. Bob Hart, who was in the cricket first XI at school, made a perfect catch but when he saw what he was holding, he dropped it as if it was red hot. It lay on the ground grinning back up at them, and the three gathered around to stare at it in a wonderful mixture of terror and excitement. Bob jumped down to join them.'

'I bet it's a woman,' said Fred.

'How can you tell that?' demanded Tom.

'It's got bits of long hair hanging off it. And anyway, it's still got its mouth open.' Fred's greatest pleasure was listening to Tommy Handley on the wireless.

'What are we going to do with it?' asked Bob Hart. This was a conundrum. Having a fox's skull or even that of a badger in their bedroom might win approval, but a human skull would lead to questions. If it came out that they had been trespassing, they could get into serious trouble.

'I'll put it back,' said Bob Farmer. Reluctantly the others agreed that this was the best policy. After they had all taken a long last look, Bob went back up the tree and dropped it into the dark hollow of the bole. When the four were reunited on the ground they swore fearsome oaths that they would never speak of what they had seen there. Then they went home for tea.

That night the nightmares came. Tom woke up screaming. He had dreamt that the grinning skull was chasing him through Hagley Woods. It had almost caught up with him when he woke up. His father came into the room, the candle in his hand giving his face a terrifying leer.

'What's wrong, boy?'

Tom was ashamed of waking his parents, but he was also overburdened by the thought of the skull. It all came out. The next morning Tom was taken to the police station by his father and made to tell the whole story again, this time to a burly desk sergeant. After being warned about the dangers of wasting police time, he was made to take a constable to the wood and show him the tree. When the constable looked into the hollow trunk, all hell broke loose.

It was not just a skull the police found, but a whole skeleton complete with shoes, fragments of clothing and a cheap wedding ring. Further searches found the skeleton's missing left hand buried nearby. The subsequent post-mortem confirmed Fred's suspicions that it was indeed female. She had died about eighteen months before and been buried in the tree soon after death, because if rigor mortis had set in, she would never have fitted into the hollow of the trunk. Some taffeta found in the mouth suggested to the pathologist that she had been asphyxiated. The labels of her clothing had been removed.

Because of distinctive irregularities of the lower jaw, the police were confident that contacting local dentists would provide them with her identity, but none of the local ones had any patients that matched that description. Even a notice in a national dental magazine produced no further clues. For all the publicity the macabre find had produced, only one man came forward with anything useful. He was a local businessman who had been walking home one evening in July 1941 when he had heard screaming coming from the woods. He had met a schoolteacher coming the other way who confirmed that he had also heard it. The police had been informed, but a search had found nothing. Now, however, it might point to the time that the unfortunate woman met her fate.

Further police enquiries were hampered by the fact that there was a war on; many people were away from their homes and therefore would not be readily missed. They came to the conclusion that it was probably someone who had tried to get away from the Birmingham Blitz and met someone she should not have.

Then events took a more sinister turn. Professor Margaret Murray of London University, a respected folklorist, let it be known that it bore all the signs of a black magic execution. Presumably this was a member of a local coven who had transgressed some law and suffered the ultimate punishment.

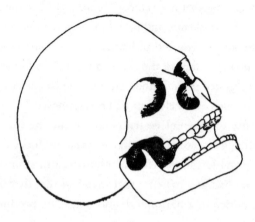

This was clearly indicated by the severing of the left hand and its burial in a separate place. Everyone knew that the Hand of Glory, taken from an executed criminal, possessed great magical powers and putting the body in a tree would prevent the spirit of the dead causing further harm. The police declined to comment.

But this proved a case that would not go away. In 1944 a mysterious graffito was written on a wall in Birmingham: 'Who put Luebella down the Wych Elm – Hagley Wood?' These kept appearing though the wording changed, eventually settling on: 'Who put Bella in the Wych Elm?' Police appealed to the writer to come forward if they had any new information, but to no avail.

Then, in November 1953, Lt-Col Wilfred Byford-Jones, a regular columnist for the *Wolverhampton Express and Star*, received a mysterious letter. It purported to explain the real reason why Bella was put in the tree, and it seemed no less fanciful than Margaret Murray's. It claimed that there had been a spy ring operating in the area during 1941, passing the location of munitions factories to the Germans. A Dutch woman got the information from a British officer and then gave it to her contact, a trapeze artist. For some reason there had been a dispute and the trapeze artist had killed the woman and placed the body in the tree. The letter even went so far as to name the British officer involved, who had died insane in 1943. The woman was named as Clarabella Donkers. Curiously, subsequent enquiries found that a Dutchman named Johannes Donkers had been executed for espionage in December 1942. Rumours of an establishment cover-up were further fuelled when it was discovered that the skeleton had mysteriously disappeared.

The police, however, were more convinced by a more prosaic solution. Around the right time, a barmaid at the nearby Gypsy's Tent pub, since renamed the Badger's Sett Tavern, had become pregnant, supposedly by one of the American troops stationed in the locality. She had left the area and it was assumed she had gone back to her parents, but the police now suspected that the G.I. had in fact killed her and hidden the body in the tree. Since she had not been called Bella it was assumed that the graffiti artist might be in league with the killer and using the name to throw the police off the scent. As soon as this story became known, people started claiming that they had seen Bella's unquiet ghost at the pub. It was this explanation that was used by Simon Holt when he made an opera on the subject.

Whatever the reason for the murder, supernatural, political or sordidly humdrum, it remains unsolved. The words, 'Who put Bella in the Wych Elm?' were last sprayed on Wychbury Obelisk, near Stourbridge, also on Lord Cobham's land, in August 1999. Was this from someone who really knew the answer, or by a vandal who knew his local history?

BIBLIOGRAPHY

Allies, Jebez, *On the Ancient British, Roman and Saxon Antiquities and Folklore of Worcestershire* (Forgotten Books, 1840).

Briggs, Katherine, *A Dictionary of British Folk-Tales* (Routledge & Kegan Paul, 1971)

Brooks, J.A., *Ghosts and Witches of the Cotswolds* (Jarrold Books, 1986)

Geoffrey of Monmouth, trans. Lewis Thorpe, *The History of the Kings of Britain* (Penguin, 1973)

Grice, Frederick, *Folk Tales of the West Midlands* (Nelson & Sons, 1952)

Jones, Lavender, *Customs and Folklore of Worcestershire* (Estragon, 1970)

Lawrence-Smith, Kathleen, *Tales of Old Worcestershire* (Countryside Books, 1989)

Lupton, Hugh, *Dreaming of Place* (Society for Storytelling, 2001)

Palmer, Roy, *The Folklore of Hereford and Worcester* (Logaston Press, 1992)

Yeates, Stephen, *A Dreaming for the Witches* (Oxbow Books, 2009)